EPISCOPACY IN THE
METHODIST TRADITION

Episcopacy in the Methodist Tradition

PERSPECTIVES AND PROPOSALS

RUSSELL E. RICHEY AND
THOMAS EDWARD FRANK

Abingdon Press
Nashville

EPISCOPACY IN THE METHODIST TRADITION: PERSPECTIVES AND PROPOSALS

Copyright © 2004 by Abingdon Press

This book is printed on acid-free paper.

Library of Congress Cataloging-in-Publication Data

Richey, Russell E.
  Episcopacy in the Methodist tradition : perspectives and proposals /
Russell E. Richey and Thomas Edward Frank.
    p. cm.
Includes bibliographical references.
  ISBN 0-687-03861-8 (alk. paper)
    1. Methodist Church—United States—Bishops—Appointment, call, and
election—History. 2. Methodist Church—United
States—Government—History. I. Frank, Thomas Edward. II. Title.

  BX8345.R53 2004
  262'.1276—dc22

                                                            2003021880

Scripture quotations are from the *New Revised Standard Version of the Bible,* copyright 1989, by the Division of Christian Education of the National Council of the Churches of Christ in the United States of America. Used by permission. All rights reserved.

04 05 06 07 08 09 10 11 12 13—10 9 8 7 6 5 4 3 2 1
MANUFACTURED IN THE UNITED STATES OF AMERICA

To our fathers, McMurry S. Richey
and Eugene M. Frank

CONTENTS

ACKNOWLEDGMENTS

Russell Richey is primarily responsible for the introduction and chapters 2 and 3; Thomas Frank for chapters 1 and 4 and the proposals of Part 2. This venture draws on previous efforts by both of us, most notably, Thomas Edward Frank, *Polity, Practice, and the Mission of The United Methodist Church*, updated edition (Nashville: Abingdon Press, 2002). Portions of chapter 1 are adapted from Frank's article, "The Discourse of Leadership and the Practice of Administration," *Journal of Religious Leadership* 1, no. 1 (Spring 2002): 1-15. A version of chapter 2, "Episcopacy in Methodism: Shadows of John Wesley," was given by Richey at the Spring 2003 "Wesley in America" conference at Perkins School of Theology. The following Richey essays have been drawn upon and the authors thank the copyright holders for permission to reproduce or echo portions thereof: "The Legacy of Francis Asbury: The Teaching Office in Episcopal Methodism," *Quarterly Review* 15 (Summer 1995): 145-74; "Francis Asbury: A Wandering Arminian," *The Historical Trail*, 1997; "Francis Asbury, James O'Kelly and Methodism's Growing Pains," *Southeastern Jurisdiction Historical Society Proceedings*, 2001; *Virginia United Methodist Heritage* 27 (Fall 2001): 24-40; *University and Church: Notes on the Methodist Experience*, published by the Office of the President, Emory University, copyright Richey © 2002, 24 pp. We also gratefully acknowledge information about the Council of Bishops' proposal for a presidency provided by Bishops Jack M. Tuell, William B. Oden, Larry M. Goodpaster, and G. Lindsey Davis.

INTRODUCTION

Richey·

I really !!! Episcopate leaders·

Episcopacy is a central feature of Methodism. The United Methodist Church (UMC) needs more than ever for its bishops to exercise an effective leadership role. The two of us believe the Church is failing to realize the full potential of this office. Our book is intended to provoke discussion and test proposals for how to bring the "itinerant general superintendency" protected in the "plan" of the Church's constitution to full expression on behalf of the Church's ministries in the world.

This book originated from a desire to provide United Methodists with helpful perspectives on the current proposal by the Council of Bishops to establish the position of Council president. The book goes to press after the Judicial Council ruled that proposal unconstitutional and before the range of General Conference legislative options on this matter have become clear. Its first purpose is to provide background for the up-and-coming discussion at General Conference about the nature of our leadership. More generally and for the longer term, it examines the perceived need for organizational change, implications of possible reorganization of the Council of Bishops, and other ways of strengthening the office. It does so by examining what Methodists have meant organizationally and theologically by the words "itinerant general superintendent," how those three words have functioned individually and together in "our plan" of episcopacy protected in the Restrictive Rules of the United Methodist (UM) constitution, and how the words have shaped or found expression in various leadership styles and forms of episcopacy through the years.

[handwritten: Osc's book / Evangelical / the ?work of 2004]

This volume will discuss the current polity of the Council and episcopacy in the Church more generally, and explore concerns about leadership that have given rise to the new proposals. It acknowledges the ambivalence some North American United Methodists have about authoritative leaders generally, but also the aspirations many now feel for stronger guidance from our bishops. In a constructive part, summarized briefly below, the book will lay out several proposals for episcopal organization and practice (with advantages and disadvantages), and explore how each gives expression to itinerant general superintendency. We will indicate whether such models or proposals have broader implications for the structure and work of the Church, note the degree to which they are in concert with the *Book of Discipline of The United Methodist Church*, and suggest where given models require changes in the *Discipline*.

Our intent, then, is to open possibilities and raise questions. The book constitutes something of a thought experiment. It does not intend to prescribe an agenda for General Conference or the Council of Bishops, but to explore ways that four aspects of Methodist episcopacy (itinerant, general, superintending, and the plan thereof) can be realized more fully.

What? Another Book About United Methodist Bishops?

The browsing or casual reader rightly might question the need for another assessment of Methodist episcopacy. Books by and about individual bishops continue to flow from the press,[1] as also general treatments of the office. In 2003, James K. Mathews and William B. Oden produced a sourcebook of episcopal statements, *Vision and Supervision*.[2] Only a couple of years prior, James E. Kirby contributed his historical overview, *The Episcopacy in American Methodism*.[3] Our effort does not aspire to the comprehensive treatment of the Council's work or the history of the office achieved by those two and similar works.[4] Rather, prompted by the recent proposal of the Council of Bishops (Council) for a four-year presidency of their body, this essay focuses sharply on the uniqueness of the United Methodist doctrine of episcopacy—itinerant general superintendency—and asks how such proposals might more fully actualize the promise in our doctrine.

In our judgment, the four-year presidency invites our reconsideration of the theological promise lodged in the constitutional protection accorded our episcopacy since 1808. In that year, the Methodist Episcopal Church stipulated in its Restrictive Rules that:

> The general conference shall have full powers to make rules and regulations for our church, under the following limitations and restrictions, viz.
>
> They shall not change or alter any part of rule of our government, so as to do away Episcopacy or destroy the plan of our itinerant general superintendency.

That quaint language, slightly revised over the years, gave constitutional protection to the episcopal leadership, including that established by the 1939 Methodist Church (unification of the Methodist Episcopal Church; Methodist Episcopal Church, South; and Methodist Protestant Church) and that established in 1968 in The United Methodist Church (Evangelical United Brethren and Methodist unification). Since the present mode of episcopacy roots most deeply in the 1808 Methodist Episcopal "Constitution" and in the traditions of leadership that it encapsulated, we will focus on that organizational stream, one that takes us back to Francis Asbury and John Wesley.

Having the spring of our episcopacy in John Wesley and its main stream through Francis Asbury, we as Methodists have, with much justification, understood and interpreted our episcopacy biographically. We have narrated episcopacy as the story of our bishops. That biographical or narrative access to the nature and evolution of itinerant general superintendency can, and sometimes has, given us theological insight into the office. Telling its story can be a powerful way of reading the office theologically. Indeed, much is now made of narrative as a way of doing theology. However, narrative can also skirt theological issues and has a way of coming to terms with whatever direction life takes, of glossing all evolution as natural, of letting operations, activities, and developments be their own justification.

Contemporary proposals that represent a significant new departure in episcopacy cannot be handled only operationally, pragmatically, or tactically. Potentially a more permanent office of presiding bishop could change power realities, not just within the Council, but between the Council and General Conference, and between the Council and our general agencies. Such practical concerns—operational, pragmatic, tactical— must, of necessity, be treated. We would suggest, however, that the proposals also provide us an opportunity to revisit the vision of itinerant general superintendency and to probe the theological possibilities and implications that another chapter of our Wesleyan narrative might open.

We do presume that the bishops, acting in Council over the last two decades, have moved to brake the movement toward a more localized form of episcopacy, the seemingly diocesan direction that the Church has steadily taken over the last century or century and a half. It is our conviction that this recent countermovement, represented in teaching and missional initiatives in the Council—in a heightened sense of the episcopacy as a teaching office, in episcopal eagerness to seek the Church's unity (both within and without), in concern over leadership and its mechanics, and in the style of our conferences—already gives fresh possibilities for itinerant general superintendency.[5] Yet this countermovement, with much of its focus within the Council, has, we believe, still a long way to go in making itinerant general superintendency the reality for the active bishops, acting in individual capacity. With respect to individual bishops and their work, the longer momentum seemingly still has power to localize and fragment. One might argue, in fact, that the longer momentum has broken apart the terms by which we describe the office and given each its discrete task:

> So bishops superintend in conference, most in only one conference, their supervision limited to the bounds of their jurisdiction or central conference, making their ordering indeed local, regional, even diocesan.
> So bishops exercise their teaching or word or general responsibility through roles in council, a collective rather than personal witness.[6]
> So bishops remain itinerant by virtue of participation in general boards and agencies, through their global visitations, and through their presence in one another's conferences.[7]

By localized or diocesan superintendency, general *episkopē* or oversight[8] in Council, and itinerating on agency assignment, United Methodist bishops live and work with the three dimensions of the episcopal office but as a fragmentation or fracturing of their fundamental calling embodied in "the plan," or so we hypothesize.[9]

This volume asks whether contemporary episcopacy could be enhanced and reformed by a clearer grounding in its unique and original conception. Could itinerant general superintendency's promise be more fully realized? And could it be realized, insofar as possible, both with respect to the Council as a whole and to the individual bishops whom we call to exercise itinerant general superintendency?

Proposals

In April 2003, the Judicial Council ruled (No. 961) that a constitutional amendment will be necessary in order to set aside a bishop for a term of four years as Council of Bishops president. We want to take the occasion of this constitutional attention to episcopacy to pursue and advocate a more general assessment of our *episkopē*. If "itinerant general superintendency" really captures the genius of our missional vision of the episcopacy, how might the office now be conceived, both with respect to its authority and exercise by individual bishops and in the Council on behalf of the whole?

We propose four "thought experiments," one predicated upon a different reading of the constitution than that adopted by the Judicial Council, others requiring disciplinary or constitutional change. The "thought experiments" we introduce immediately below so as to anticipate our constructive proposals and to encourage readers to move around the volume as they feel the need, some perhaps moving first to the proposals and then back to the chapters that provide context and background.

Each of the proposals accents one of the terms of the Methodist doctrine of *episkopē*. Each evokes at least one basic rubric of the order of elder to which bishops are ordained. Each recalls one dimension of Christ's office. Each reminds us of or anticipates an aspect of Francis Asbury's exercise of leadership, discussed schematically in chapter 3. These connections—to one of the terms of our plan of itinerant general superintendency; to one of our ministerial rubrics (service, Word, sacrament, order); or to one dimension of Christ's office (servant, prophet, priest, king)—remind us that in thinking about episcopacy we open up fundamental-theological and practical-theological issues. Though we accent one of the above connectives with each proposal, in fact, all are inseparably linked in the import and exercise of the episcopal office. Our purpose, to reiterate, is to suggest that changes in superintendency have great theological and practical significance. And the proposals below and in part 2, collectively and each in particular, we offer as potentially for the well-being of our connection as a whole as especially for the exercise within it of *episkopē*.

"General" Election

Our first proposal is that the body that alone is empowered to speak for the Church, General Conference, once again elect bishops. Election there would make bishops symbolically "itinerant general superintendents" of a global Church. It would encourage the delegates to think about the general needs of the denomination in their balloting and might elicit candidacies whose experience and talents have already been tested on a churchwide basis. It would make more thinkable appointment on a connectional basis, and in a variety of ways could enhance the cross fertilization that broader episcopal deployment and exchanges permit.

By making bishops clearly servants of the entire Church, this proposal corresponds, we suggest, with "the plan" part of our "plan of our itinerant general superintendency." It also underscores the connectional *service* that the bishops individually and collectively have committed themselves to in their various episcopal initiatives, most dramatically in that on children and poverty. It evokes memories of Francis Asbury's dramatic initiative in demanding the convening of a general conference of the preachers to exercise an elective role in the selection of bishops for the Church and the necessity thereafter of such a general gathering for episcopal elections. And, of course, "service" now identified as one of the four basic ministerial rubrics points us unmistakably to him who models our leadership, Christ the suffering servant.

Itinerant Presidency

After General Conference has completed the task of electing the number of bishops required to fill vacancies, plus one, and before episcopal assignments are made, our second proposal looks at how General Conference might elect one of the active bishops as president of the Council of Bishops with release from the residential duties of an episcopal area; or the president may, as in the Council proposal tested in Judicial Council, be elected by the Council.

Should the Church select this pattern of a "set-aside" bishop as president of the Council, it might wish to cast an eye to the Episcopal Church for some understanding of such an office and its most effective usage. It might also find helpful the disciplinary language on representation removed in 1996. "Representation" or "representative ministry," employed in the *Disciplines* from 1976 to 1996, nicely captures the *sacramental* potential of a presidential office. A presidency conceived and authorized as representative and sacramental might reflect itinerancy in interesting fashion. Through itinerancy on behalf of the Council's "general oversight and promotion of the spiritual and temporal interests of the entire Church" (¶ 45), the president would be a constant presence and a symbolic representation of the connection as a whole. The president of the Council would, indeed, be present for United Methodism and for the Council in those places requiring ceremonial or official representation.

The Council would acquire its needed administrative leadership in this pattern, as the president guides the Council's work. Indeed, a Council presidency would enhance the itinerant general superintendency by giving it a substance and consistency that it has lacked. It will make it more possible for the bishops to exercise their constitutional duties of oversight, by giving them a continuing organization for their work. But by accenting presidency in sacramental terms, the Church would be invited to think of the Council president, less in terms of the modern corporation's chief executive offices or on analogy with the United States presidency, than in relation to Christ's priestly office. It would be fitting that the Council president be thought of as our chief sacramental officer. He or she would itinerate across the Church, as we shall see, did Francis Asbury, the Church's first chief priest.

Whether this model would enhance the "itinerant general superintendency" of all the bishops—of the bishops individually—might depend on how fully the theology of the episcopal office is developed, whether bishops are indeed elected in general conference and if they become appointable across the connection rather than regionally or jurisdictionally. The understanding of the Council president's office as sacramental in character, and its authority as representative, might raise fewer concerns about centralization of power. A Council president who led by breaking bread or washing away sins would, in his or her exercise of the office, connect with, rather than distance himself or herself from the other bishops. And a presidency so understood might pose less operational or constitutional challenge to General Conference's right to speak for the denomination.

General Oversight of the Church's Mission

If the preceding pattern accents "itinerancy," our third proposal emphasizes the bishops' "general" responsibilities, particularly their oversight of the Church and of the Church's work. Here, too, the election of bishops by General Conference would make clearer the expectation that they exercise leadership of the whole connection.

That leadership might be expressed particularly in strengthening further the episcopal direction of the Church's boards and agencies. This proposal, with its expectation that the bishops individually and collectively undertake the planning and missional direction of the denomination, recalls Christ's prophetic office and the *Word* rubric for ministry. It builds on the Council's considerable success with teaching and missional initiatives and locates the oversight by the bishops and the Council not in a single office but in activities of the denomination's missional agencies.

Such prophetic roles, as we shall see, Asbury, along with his compatriot, Thomas Coke, exercised in early American Methodism. They were the editors-in-chief, primary policymakers of the denomination, shapers and annotators of the *Discipline*, and coordinators of the Church's work. The Restrictive Rules indeed have protected our "itinerant general superintendency," but they also substantively altered the role that Francis Asbury had played as a connectional officer and in conference affairs. Asbury had not only presided in annual and general conferences but had been the major actor, the agenda setter, the policymover, the agent of the Church's mission.

Our third thought experiment echoes other proposals to enhance the episcopal voice in and roles within general agencies and to involve bishops and perhaps the Council in the coordination of their work. Episcopal stewardship or trusteeship, already represented by presidency of boards, might involve (1) creation of task groups within the Council functioning something like congressional oversight committees; (2) establishment of other Council committees to take responsibility for coordination of denominational policy; and (3) acknowledgment of the bishops as the primary "connectors" between local and conference concerns and denominational work. Bishops and episcopal committees would thereby give even greater leadership to the Church in mission. Such roles might entail taking over some or all of the tasks currently assigned to General Council on Ministries (GCOM). Alternatively, GCOM might be thought of as a structure within the Council that functions to provide the administrative backup and coordination needed for the Council and sought by present proposals for a four-year presidency. However such assignments were organized, the Church would continue to expect the bishops to speak a needed word to the Church and to lead by symbolic action.

The bishops have been self-conscious about the importance of "conferencing" and of their role as models. This pattern extends that responsibility throughout the whole of our structure and effectively makes the bishops our "general" conferencing agents. This recovery of the episcopal voice, and of the bishops collectively and individually, accents the "general" aspect of the Methodist understanding of *episkopē*. It evokes the *Word* as a basic ordination or ministerial rubric; and it recalls the prophetic dimension of Christ's office.

Superintendency in Conferences

Our final proposal evokes Christ's royal office, *order* as ministerial or ordination rubric, and the presiding or superintending dimension of episcopacy. It recalls the preeminent role that Asbury played in setting agenda for conferences and, by his appointments, setting agenda for circuits and stations. Asbury chaired in active fashion, bringing in proposals, making motions, speaking to matters under discussion. While William McKendree's innovation of the episcopal address recalled that earlier role, it did so in quite minimal fashion. Post-1808, one might say, bishops in conference lost their voice, being expected to speak only when spoken to, that is, to preside only.

While bishops have hardly been voiceless, their presidency or chairing role might to advantage be restored to its Asburian activism. United Methodists will not, we suspect, wish to emulate our Episcopal kinfolk and transform the Council into a House of Bishops. However, we could find ways within present understandings to re-establish an active presidency for all bishops. Bishops might, for instance, preside in many more contexts than they do now and their presidency might entail far more of what inheres in such an office in most other organizational cultures. One current idea, as we understand it, is for bishops to serve as chairs of General Conference committees. In addition, the bishops in Council and in committees thereof, might as general officers of the Church receive all petitions, legislation, reforming ideas, agenda from across the connection and from the general agencies. They might establish priorities within such submissions. They might recommend how items might be aggregated or divided. In various other ways and in general, the bishops might take responsibility for the legislative agenda of the denomination and particularly of General Conference.

Of course, bishops would continue to preside in general agencies. Their enhanced activities in General Conference might be coordinated in some fashion with responsibilities in general agencies, such that bishops would be widely accorded primary spokesperson and representational roles on the Church's behalf. Those stronger connectional leadership profiles would doubtless also enrich and enhance the Council's relation to the Church's life and work. An episcopacy even stronger in its connectional leadership would bring wider denominational concerns, ideas, and resources to bear in the annual conferences, as we have seen already.

Questions for the Church

These four thought experiments, all predicated upon and each clearly demanding significant change, might serve—as the volume as a whole is intended—to invite our reflection about what our bishops can and should offer the Church in the way of leadership in the decades ahead. The call for a presidency of the Council indicates, we believe, the conviction on the part of the bishops that they can exercise more authority and give more guidance than that with which the Church currently empowers them. This volume begins with their conviction. Further we assume that significant revisioning of the episcopal office will require changes in both polity and practice. We posit that the Methodist practice of this office offers us far more in the potential for effective connectional leadership than recent trends toward regionalized or localized, even diocesan, epis-copacy now yield and therefore we revisit the foundations of Methodist episcopacy.

Chapter 1 frames our queries about bishops by analyzing what the Church has been saying to itself about leadership, episcopal leadership in particular. Chapter 2 contrasts the American Methodist understanding of "itinerant general superintendency" with other options prevalent and available when the Church was founded. Chapter 3 exhibits the embod-iment of that understanding in the superintendency of Francis Asbury and indicates how the Church thereafter struggled to hold the three dimensions of *episkopē* together. Chapter 4 moves to the present, to the exercise of itinerant general superintendency, and to the various con-straints thereon. Part 2 lays out the four proposals or thought experiments briefly sketched already. Having entertained proposals concerning the office of bishop that would dramatically change the Church, we conclude by encouraging the 2004 General Conference to be cautious, and to probe even more deeply into the office of bishop, most immediately through the creation of a General Conference study commission to bring proposals for reform to the 2008 session.

Notes

1. A partial list from our own shelves includes: L. Bevel Jones III, *One Step Beyond Caution: Reflections on Life and Faith* (Decatur, Ga.: Looking Glass Books, 2001); James E. Kirby, *Brother Will: A Biography of William C. Martin* (Nashville: Abingdon Press, 2000); *A Global Odyssey: The Autobiography of James K. Mathews* (Nashville: Abingdon Press, 2000); James C. Logan, *A Charge to Keep: The Life of Earl Gladstone Hunt Jr.* (Nashville: Abingdon Press, 2000); William R. Cannon, *A Magnificent Obsession: The Autobiography of William Ragsdale Cannon,* foreword by Earl G. Hunt Jr. (Nashville: Abingdon Press, 1999); Robert Moats Miller, *Bishop G. Bromley Oxnam: Paladin of Liberal Protestantism* (Nashville: Abingdon Press, 1990); and *Ninety Years and Counting: Autobiography of Nolan B. Harmon* (Nashville: The Upper Room, 1983).

2. For insights into the episcopal office and particularly into the exercise of *episkopē* [on this concept see the reference in note 8] within the Council of Bishops, see James K. Mathews and William B. Oden, eds., *Vision and Supervision: A Sourcebook of Significant Documents of the Council of Bishops of The United Methodist Church* (Nashville: Abingdon Press, 2003).

3. James E. Kirby, *The Episcopacy in American Methodism* (Nashville: Abingdon Press/Kingswood, 2000).

4. See the various United Methodist essays in Jack M. Tuell and Roger W. Fjeld, eds., *Episcopacy: Lutheran-United Methodist Dialogue II* (Minneapolis: Augsburg, 1991). For other published explorations of episcopacy, see notes below and in subsequent chapters.

5. See Mathews and Oden, eds., *Vision and Supervision: A Sourcebook,* the whole of which illustrates this trend. For explicit treatment of changes in the Council, see section IX, "Presidential Addresses," and especially those by Emilio J. M. DeCarvalho, Woodie W. White, George W. Bashore, and William B. Oden, pp. 536-69.

6. See Roy H. Short, *History of The Council of Bishops of The United Methodist Church, 1939–1979* (Nashville: Abingdon Press, 1980).

7. On the several roles and how bishops exercise them, see James K. Mathews, *Set Apart to Serve: The Meaning and Role of Episcopacy in the Wesleyan Tradition* (Nashville: Abingdon Press, 1985). On the exercise of the roles by individual bishops, see recent biographies or autobiographies noted previously (note 1).

8. On the notion of *episkopē* as oversight see "The Nature and Purpose of the Church: A Stage on the Way to a Common Statement," Faith and Order Paper No. 181—November 1998. World Council of Churches, Faith and Order: http://www.wcc-coe.org/wcc/what/faith/nature.html. "Oversight: Communal, Personal and Collegial": "The Church as the body of Christ and the eschatological people of God is built up by the Holy Spirit through a diversity of gifts or ministries. Among these gifts a ministry of *episkopē* (oversight) serves to express and promote the visible unity of the body. Every church needs this ministry of unity in some form." The seventeen paragraphs that follow develop the various dimensions of episcopal oversight.

See also section III. The Forms of the Ordained Ministry in "Baptism, Eucharist and Ministry," Faith and Order Paper No. 111; copyright 1982 World Council of Churches, 30th printing, 1996: http://www.wcc-coe.org/wcc/what/faith/bem5.html.

9. We also hypothesize, though we cannot develop here this assumption fully or explore its implications, that itinerant general superintendency's fracturing has been accelerated

by the adoption in the 1939 union of the jurisdictional system. That system has nurtured a regionalism and localism feared by opponents of the 1939 jurisdictional arrangement. Itinerant general superintendency breaks apart, its disintegration being probably accelerated, certainly not inhibited, by jurisdictional selection and deployment and exercise. Some serious reconsideration of the jurisdictional system may be in order, if the Church comes to share our concern for the reclamation of the three dimensions of episcopacy as promise, expectation, and possibility in the life and work of each and every bishop.

PART ONE

Perspectives

Frank

CHAPTER ONE

Bishops as Leaders

Expectations, Realities, and Possibilities

The central question of our essay is how to enhance the episcopal office for the work most needed in the Church today. But United Methodists generally exhibit little interest in the actual office of bishop within the traditions and polity of Methodism. The Church has had relatively little recent discussion of the constitutional powers and duties of bishops, the last study of the subject commissioned by General Conference having been completed nearly thirty years ago. On the other hand, United Methodists express many concerns for the Church and hopes for what bishops might be able to do about them. They look to the bishops for leadership in meeting the Church's challenges.

Calls for episcopal leadership have been a constant refrain in the life of The United Methodist Church. The terms "leader" or "leadership" scarcely appeared in the 1960–1964 study of the episcopacy for The Methodist Church.[1] Yet Bishop Roy Short's 1985 history and biography of bishops was titled *The Episcopal Leadership Role in United Methodism*, with chapter titles using language such as "Episcopal Leadership Team" and "Exercising a Group Leadership Role Today."[2] Evidently something in the history and social context of the UMC brought leadership language to the foreground.

Certainly the UMC has confronted significant change in its own institutions and in the societies around it. The creation of the denomination in 1968 was a huge and complex task of church union, and it occurred right at the time of immense changes in U.S. society and in global economics and politics. The denomination was new in a new era marked by the end of Western colonialism, the advances of civil rights laws in the U.S., and rapid cultural change in gender roles, sexuality, and the arts. Many people have expected that the bishops would lead the way toward answers to the perplexing challenges and institutional adjustments that face the Church. "In a church that is overmanaged and underled, we desperately need our bishops to become leaders in the decentralization and creation of a new connection," insists Andy Langford and William Willimon in their 1995 manifesto for A *New Connection: Reforming The United Methodist Church.*[3] In the view of many laity, pastors, and denominational executives, only strong, effective leadership from the bishops can enable the Church to confront its problems and realize its possibilities.

The call for episcopal leadership is part of a broader crisis of leadership portrayed especially by those who view the UMC's thirty-five-year history as a narrative of decline, failure, and irrelevance. In countless books, articles, speeches, and sermons, United Methodist authors and speakers have recounted such woes as the steady loss of gross national church membership in the U.S., the growth of a bloated bureaucracy of general agencies for ministry and mission, and the Church's failure to attract able candidates to its ordained ministries. The fact that church membership and affiliation statistics are notoriously difficult to manage and interpret meaningfully, that the general agencies are limping by with a fraction of the staff necessary to carry out their General Conference mandates, and that UM seminaries for the most part have full enrollments, cannot stand up to the rhetorical tide of crisis talk. Given the assumption of crisis, the leaders at the top—the bishops—are crucial figures in turning things around.

The crisis rhetoric of the UMC expresses a common theme across U.S. society. Particularly in times of stock market downturn, rising unemployment, and corporate layoffs, people begin to ask, "Where have all the leaders gone?" As one professor of management put it, "When people are in crisis, they want others to comfort them and take a visible role in ending the crisis." In the words of an executive headhunter, "The hunger for leadership is greater in a tough economy . . . people want leaders who can pull them out of the wilderness to better times."[4]

This widely perceived "crisis of leadership" in U.S. corporations, institutions, government, and even families has spawned a whole industry of "leadership"—institutes, grant programs, conferences, consultants, Web sites, and thousands of books, journals, and articles. Americans are fascinated by powerful corporate executives and entrepreneurs such as Jack Welch, retired CEO of General Electric, and seek to learn the secrets of "leadership" that lead to "success."[5] Anyone who does anything noteworthy—Rudolph Giuliani, Colin Powell, Vince Lombardi—merits a book on "leadership."[6] Most leadership books and seminars focus on the traits of effective leaders (of course, a leader by definition is effective or she or he would not be identified as a leader). Some look to Jesus or other biblical figures for the traits—digested from the Scripture as *Leading by the Book* or *Jesus CEO*—thus giving "leadership" a nimbus of divine approval.[7] The implication in much leadership literature is that if one simply adopts the traits or attributes deduced from the stories of great men (and the figures profiled are almost always men), one can become a leader.

As United Methodists prepare to elect and assign their bishops in 2004, they might want especially to have a look at Rakesh Khurana's recent study of corporate CEO searches. Many boards of business corporations, trying to please the often unreasonable expectations of stockholders for immediate gains in stock values, have been looking eagerly for "corporate saviors"—individuals who can "singlehandedly sav[e] a troubled corporation." These "messiahs" are often hired without regard to their actual experience in the particular business's product, but appear to have the "charisma" or "traits" expected of an "aggressive" leader. Needless to say, many corporate boards have been disappointed at the inability of their hired "stars" to connect with the organization. A similar issue in the Church is evident in the remark of one bishop interviewed by Judith Smith for her study of leadership challenges in the episcopacy: "People want bishops to wave their magic wand and fix it all—an attitude that prevents creative, mutual work."[8]

The Discourse of Leadership in the UMC

The proliferation of leadership discourse in the churches and larger society forces the UMC to define more carefully what it means by the terms "leader" and "leadership." The Church has been no more discerning about this than any other organization. *The Book of Discipline 2000*, for example, makes the first responsibility of bishops listed in ¶ 414 a mandate "to lead." The vocation of "servant leadership" is designated for all the ministries of the Church (¶¶ 136-137, 319, 325, 404.1, etc.). But nowhere does the Church define what it means by "leadership" or more particularly "servant leadership."

A compelling reason for the Church to avoid such definitions is that saying what leadership is would expose the confusion of multiple purposes that typifies contemporary churches. The discourse of leadership reflects the intentions of an organization. No one is called a leader unless she or he is helping the organization fulfill its purposes. So to define leadership is to state more clearly those purposes and how they relate to each other. In fact, calls for leadership often accompany efforts to assert one particular organizational purpose over others, with leadership a symbolic word standing for the emergent dominance of that purpose.

Recent UMC history offers two clear examples. The 1996 General Conference adopted the church growth slogan of "making disciples of Jesus Christ" as a mission statement for the denomination. This action followed a general social trend in the U.S. of business corporations, government agencies, and institutions devising mission statements to declare publicly their purpose and aims. The phrase was inserted into the *Discipline* as a mandate for every office and governing body of the Church. The introductory paragraph in the episcopacy chapter (¶ 401) was altered to include the statement, "The mission of the Church is to make disciples of Jesus Christ," followed after an intervening sentence by a claim that, "The purpose of superintending is to equip the Church in its disciple-making ministry."

Since the *Discipline* now advocates an organizational system for "making" more disciples (esp. ¶ 122), clearly the operative framework here is church as productive enterprise. Leadership for productivity requires initiative, innovation, and strategic planning that will lead to growing numbers of members and churches. Effective leadership will bring growth. Many bishops have taken this mandate to heart, challenging, cajoling, and encouraging the conferences over which they preside to start more congregations in newly developing areas and seek growth in existing ones. Citing Wesley's own preoccupation with numbers, they put statistical reports (even quarterly reports just like corporate CEOs) front and

28

One can be honored with numbers

center in clergy meetings and conferences. They measure their own success as a bishop by whether their conference's numbers are growing.

The 1996 General Conference also adopted the language of "servant leadership" as a descriptor for every office of ministry, including bishops. The bishops are now authorized for their episcopal role "as followers of Jesus Christ called to servant leadership" (¶ 404.1). Presumably this term, also widely used in U.S. corporations and institutions, advocates service to some higher purpose. It suggests service to larger organizational purposes that advance the common good not only of the organization but of the wider community and society. The leader is to direct her or his attention to the organization's contribution to the common welfare, and to subject himself or herself to whatever is needed to reach these purposes.[9] As growing numbers of organizations have adopted the term, it has shifted as well toward a focus on internal administrative styles and values. The servant leader abjures autocratic action and advances broad participation in goal setting and consensus models of decision making.

The churches would seem to be a natural home for models of servant leadership, many of which are grounded explicitly in religious traditions. The Church's higher purpose can be plainly defined as witness of the kingdom of God, with Jesus Christ as exemplar of service to the kingdom, and the Church's organizational practices viewed as potential signs of what God's kingdom is like. What servant leadership means specifically for a bishop remains unclear, however. Many bishops emphasize the Church's inclusiveness and strive to get as many voices to the table of decision making as possible. Many have experimented with consensus models in preference to the parliamentary procedures of Robert's Rules of Order, even in large annual conference assemblies. Yet management scholars warn that servant leadership can reduce a leader to being "a conduit for the desires of followers," her or his "service" more like a deferral to the wishes of whatever group is dominant in the organization. This is particularly an issue for women in official roles, from whom many men expect deference anyway.[10] The longer the term remains an undefined ideal, the more it can mask the realities of power relations in the Church and become a tool for dominance by ideological parties or assertive personalities.

In striking ways these two recently adopted terms carry contrasting and complementary expectations for leadership. "Making disciples" as a mission slogan emphasizes aggression, territoriality, and gain. "Servant leadership" as a style for conducting an office emphasizes consensus, humility, and self-giving. The Church seems to be declaring that it expects both sets of traits to be balanced in its leaders.

These are only two of the competing sets of expectations for UM leaders, bishops in particular. The UMC encompasses a variety of what organizational studies scholars Roger Friedland and Robert Alford call "institutional logics." The "central logic" of an institution, they argue, is "a set of material practices and symbolic constructions [that] constitutes its organizing principles." Capitalism as a social institution is organized around the logic of accumulation and commodification. The family embraces the logic of community and loyalty.[11] Particular organizations structure themselves around central logics, but include secondary logics as well. For example, a corporation might have expanded productivity and growing market share as a central logic, but also exhibit a family-like culture of loyalty to the organization.[12]

The leadership role of UM bishops is a creature of multiple logics in the Church. As symbols of the Church's unity and continuity with the apostles, they "enable the church to worship and serve the Triune God," in Langford and Willimon's words.[13] This language resonates with the UM constitutional definition of the Church's purpose as providing "for the maintenance of worship, the edification of believers, and the redemption of the world" (Preamble, p. 21). Yet even if such wording were accepted as the central logic, many other logics are at work in shaping the role. Bishops are elected in delegate assemblies of clergy and laity—the logic of republican democracy, representation, and participation. They are asked to serve as pastor of the pastors—the logic of communal covenant and care. They are charged with oversight of the governing bodies of church agencies and institutions—the logic of corporate management and bureaucracy. They are invited to bless programs and facilities and to preach—the logic of liturgy, sacramental symbolism, and proclamation. They are mandated to lead the Church in mission—the logic of entrepreneurship and productivity. They are expected to be servant leaders—the logic of consensus and shared purpose.[14]

The *Discipline* provides little or no official guidance in how to sort out these logics. Even the 1976 General Conference approval of a chapter on episcopacy separate from the ordained ministry chapter did not illuminate matters much. Only a few lines inserted from the 1972–1976 study report on the episcopacy sketch out some of the issues of "mode, pace, skill" needed for today's bishops (¶ 402). No paragraph of the chapter or the *Discipline* offers any historical or theological rationale for episcopacy.

No paragraph describes or summarizes the practices of episcopacy in Methodist heritages. No paragraph suggests how a bishop might prioritize among tasks grounded in these multiple institutional logics. Perhaps the most pressing leadership challenge of any bishop is simply to find her or his own way forward through this tangle of competing expectations.

The Nature of Leadership

Churches have always been and will always be complex organizations with diverse purposes. The texts and stories around which churches gather for worship and witness can be interpreted in many ways and are embodied in many forms. Centuries of appeal to the model of "the New Testament church" have resulted not in uniformity or consensus, but an immense diversity of understandings of Christian community. Church structures and offices are always expressive of cultural contexts, since there is no visible church apart from its cultural incarnations. The resulting diversity of forms, understandings, and expressions even within particular traditions such as Methodism is bound to create complex expectations of organizational officers.

Rather than try to sort, prioritize, and codify the complexity of the Church and its multiple organizational logics, bishops and those who elect and work with them would be better served by a deepening sense of what people and institutions want when they call for leadership. What people seem to mean when they speak of leadership has something to do with organizational energies and purposes. Whatever the content of leadership may be, it is most fully understood as a dynamic that is contextual, communal, and systemic.

Leadership is always contextual. The term has no meaning apart from the context in which it is named, recognized, or expected. Bishops realize this immediately in everyday life. Are they still episcopal leaders when they are grocery shopping or hiking in a national park? Certainly, but no one acknowledges them as such (and they would just as soon not be recognized on vacation). Phone solicitations asking for a "Mr. or Mrs. Bishop" or puzzled looks from airplane seatmates who have asked innocently, "What do you do?" indicate the social limits within which episcopal leadership is meaningful. Leadership is inseparable from the institutional and social contexts that give it content.

More broadly, leadership is always framed by particular situations. A leader in one circumstance is not a leader in another. George W. Bush's presidency was hotly contested when he was inaugurated, but nine months later when he stood at Ground Zero in Manhattan he was widely looked to for leadership. A university president leads one school back from the brink of insolvency and instills confidence in the trustees and faculty, but goes to a seemingly more stable institution a decade later and finds herself in a swamp of power struggles and bitter divisions. A pastor who has nurtured a thriving suburban congregation and enjoys warm support for his ministry suddenly has the congregation's officers turn against him on the Sunday he invites the rabbi of a neighboring synagogue to preach.

A bishop may be extraordinarily effective in unifying ministers and churches around one cause—emergency response to hurricane damage, for example, or strategies for planting new congregations in exurban areas—but find herself unable to stir any action about another pressing issue—streamlined management of conference finances, for example. Whatever is called leadership is always contextual, arising out of circumstance and shaped by situations. No one has a formula for understanding why leadership emerges in some situations and not in others (though plenty of books promise it). Bishops simply have to employ every gift of discernment and every form of data at their disposal in order to understand what they need to do in particular contexts.

Second, whatever leadership is, it is always communal in character. Just as organizational purposes express the whole nature of an organization, so leadership expresses the direction of an organization as a corporate body. The word most often associated with leadership is "vision"—a term exploited so often in so many different ways as to have been rendered almost unusable. If what people mean by vision is something like a picture of what we want our organization to look like in the future, then clearly that vision must arise from and be widely shared in the organization. The role of leaders may be to articulate and continually remind everyone of the vision, but a leader who is sole author of the vision usually is doomed to irrelevance.

In her study of episcopal leadership based on interviews with five bishops identified by numbers of church people as "creative, visionary leaders," Smith named crucial features of shared vision. While bishops may be "stewards of the vision," the vision itself must "grow out of the community." The leader's role is to help "the community discern the vision" by striving to create a climate of discernment and receptivity. Once the vision is received and affirmed, the episcopal leader "motivates, encourages, and organizes the community to live out that vision." The picture of what the Church wants to be can only be "realized by the community not by the leader."

Moreover, vision expresses the communal character of an organization as it has evolved over time. In Smith's words, summarizing her interviews with the five bishops, "the community must understand both past and future" as it realizes its vision.[15] The Church is a steward of traditions that reach back to biblical times, and perpetuates practices that have continued in various cultural forms for over twenty centuries. Particular heritages such as Methodism embrace practices over two hundred years old. The constitutional sentence establishing the episcopacy itself has existed virtually unchanged since 1808. Yet at the same time the Church faces the challenges of an unfolding future in a world transformed by technology, development, and growing human population.

The leadership task is always to enable the people of an organization or community to adapt and thrive in changing circumstances, drawing deeply on the gifts and strengths of their heritage of purpose and practice. Helping the Church remember its history, name its character, claim its gifts, and use its resources to the full is central to episcopal leadership. The link of past and future is communal in nature, for it must be realized and affirmed by the community in order to be meaningful. The community itself must find the most effective balance of continuity with traditions and innovation for new circumstances.

In a seminar with a dozen bishops a few years ago, I suggested that we explore the contextual and communal nature of leadership through an exercise in organizational culture. I asked each bishop to bring an object that would symbolize something of the character of the annual conference(s) over which he or she presided. As we went around the table, I noted that a few bishops brought printed materials or tokens representing conference programs for evangelism and mission. But I was struck by how many bishops in the group brought something expressive of the landscape, and therefore of the people and their way of life, in the annual conferences. Here was a miniature lighthouse, and here a plastic dairy cow, a seashell and a swatch of handcrafted fabric. Each was evocative of the heritage and the contemporary challenges of life in that region.

What did these objects have to do with the Church? Blessedly, the bishops did not make them into moral object lessons about the Church's responsibilities. Instead, they let the objects show how embedded the Church is with the lives of people. The gospel was incarnate in the strug-

Context

gles and satisfactions, divisions and harmonies, of life in real human communities. The churches over which the bishops presided were fully contextual and the churches' hopes, visions, and actions communal. The bishops' role was to help them understand their context, name their particularity, realize their strengths, and embrace their picture of what they want the Church to be like in their region.

Systemic Frameworks for Interpreting Episcopal Leadership

Third, whatever leadership is, it is systemic in nature. It is a force or dynamic that is generated by the interaction of various roles and elements of an organizational system, their functions and processes. The leadership dynamic flows through an organizational system as a whole as the name for organizational movement toward corporate or communal purposes. Leadership is not meaningful apart from the system that generates it and allows it to work.

Four frameworks for understanding organizational systems are particularly helpful in analyzing and interpreting churches and the episcopal role within them. First, churches are cultural systems constructed out of varied elements of secular and religious traditions. Through the interaction of their idiom, symbols, rituals, stories, processes, values, and worldviews, churches form and reform a culture through which they express their faith. In the UMC as in other episcopal traditions, the office of bishop itself carries enormous symbolic weight in the cultural system. The bishop is a presence, an image of the Church's unity and collective authority. Lore about bishops abounds in the Church's oral traditions, and social rituals of deference and honor cluster around the office. Yet the culture of episcopacy is always interacting with other elements of the Church's culture such as the symbols and processes of conference or the regional heritage of appointive ministry, perhaps best captured in particular annual conferences as "the way we do things around here."[16]

The assignment of a bishop to an episcopal area is a shock to the cultural system already in place, no matter how familiar the bishop may seem. The system must absorb the ways and perspectives of the new bishop, and will seek a homeostasis or stability similar to what existed before the bishop arrived. Every gesture of a new bishop has cultural significance. Here is a bishop who arrives at his first cabinet meeting and greets the district superintendents, who are all standing around sipping coffee and watching him. The bishop surveys the long, rectangular table, and chooses a seat in the middle of one side. Later he learns that the tangible wave of shock that went through the group derived from the unbroken history of bishops always sitting at the head of the table. During his entire tenure, while he keeps his center seat, he still experiences the pattern of hierarchical deference to him as bishop.

Episcopal leadership for change in the Church's cultural system must be immersed in the local culture. No bishop can be truly effective without exhibiting a deep knowledge and appreciation of the laity and ordained ministers, the places, institutions, and congregations with whom he or she is working in a particular region (thus the significance of the symbols assembled in the session discussed above). Only by honoring the cultural ways of a conference can a bishop help it achieve greater knowledge of its own heritage, its unique character and strengths, and its possibilities for future ministry.

Second, churches are systems of personal and emotional relationships. Roles of authority and deference, maternalism and paternalism, affiliation and boundary setting in the relational system of the church can be usefully understood through the metaphor of "family." Persons to whom others defer can be thought of as "parents," those who defer as "children," and those who refuse to defer but still want to participate in the system as "independent children." Those who take responsibility away from others by acting on their behalf may do so paternalistically by asserting their power over them, or maternalistically by overfunctioning and taking care of everything for everybody. Persons can intervene in the system by affiliating with those who are excluded from relationship by rigid boundaries, and by setting clear boundaries of integrity and authority to avoid emotional triangles and manipulations. [17]

Bishops find themselves by virtue of office in a "parental" role, the object of deference and distancing across the parental authority boundary. They are alone and without peers except for other parent-bishops like themselves and often their spouses who stand beside them in the family structure (sometimes as their surrogate). Many bishops complain that because of their parent role no one tells them the truth; few really believe the compliments lavished on them. The leadership challenge for them is to find ways to reduce the distance and to nurture the family-like system of the churches under their care toward full maturity of communication and adult generativity.

The psychology of the nurturing task is subtle and complex, and understanding it requires patience and savvy. The bishop can be projected by the community into the role not only of parent, but also of collective "ego," expected to organize the "self" of a conference for meaningful tasks that create identity and purpose. Since conferences are comprised of diverse interests, locales, and personalities, functioning in a continually changing environment, to build a collective identity is a challenge that can easily become a bishop's preoccupation. Too easily the bishop can paternalistically assert himself as the personification of a conference's identity, or maternalistically overfunction to try to give the conference an identity it does not claim for itself. Bishops must be aware of the community's projection and their own response, in order to deflect ego needs shrewdly into forms that will help the community grow its own ego strengths. Otherwise, she may find herself the object of public admiration and private rage as the community passive-aggressively compensates for its self-perceived lack of identity.[18]

A third view of church organizations understands them as systems of productivity. Through their core processes, organizations such as churches carry out their primary task, receiving inputs of people and resources and producing outputs that have an impact beyond the production system itself. The *Discipline* describes this system in the UMC as seeking, welcoming, and gathering "persons into the body of Christ," leading them "to commit their lives to God," nurturing them "in Christian living," sending them into the world to live in love and justice, and continuing the process by inviting others into the community of faith (¶ 122). If the mission is to make more and more disciples of Christ, the primary task is to form people through core processes of seeking, welcoming, educating, and equipping persons for a life of faith.

The episcopal role in the Church as productivity system is primarily articulation of the mission toward which the system aims, and management and enhancement of the elements that make the system more effective. Thus bishops are preachers and teachers who proclaim and interpret the faith traditions into which people are to be formed. Bishops are charged with discerning the gifts of the people under their appointment and placing them in situations where they can be most effective. Bishops are exemplars of the Church's mission, not only advocating it but also putting themselves in the places of greatest need in order to focus the system's attention on new challenges.

Bishops are regularly criticized or warned about becoming "managers" of the Church's system instead of its "leaders." This distinction—widespread in the literature of all organizations in the United States—assumes that management attends only to keeping the machinery running, while leadership expresses new directions and visions.[19] But this is a specious distinction, showing once again that talk of leadership is another way of advocating change or even masking programs for change being pushed by one group or another in the Church. The system cannot function without wise and knowledgeable management by the persons charged with offices of oversight. If management refers to the responsible use of funds, the full participation of interested parties in decision making, and the appropriate placement of persons for their work, then surely management is a critical task for bishops.

The greater risk in the contemporary dynamics of church as productivity system is that the bishop will take on the role of chief executive officer of the annual conference organization. The more the rhetoric of crisis is used to leverage adoption of goals and programs for church growth, the more bishops are pushed—or choose to fit—into a position at the top of a production pyramid. As CEOs they would be authors of conference goals, the executive to which all other ministers report their progress, and the final office of approval for all programs and budgets. Some conferences have moved perilously close to such a model, but bishops should firmly reject it. By tradition, polity, and practice, ministry and mission in United Methodism is a communal, conference enterprise and should remain so.

Mention of polity brings us to the fourth view of church organizations, as political systems of power and authority. Churches as diverse human communities are by nature political. They must weigh the interests of varied constituencies and make choices about their use of resources. In order to achieve a measure of stability and consistency in self-governance, they devise constitutions that assign powers and duties on behalf of the community. They create offices to which the community grants authority—power legitimated by the community—for carrying out responsibilities for the good of the whole. At the same time, much power in all organizations—the ability to get things done—remains informal, exercised by charismatic individuals, aggressive interest groups, or simply persons to whom others defer.

What people mean by leadership does not necessarily coincide with office. Leadership may be spread broadly in a healthy organization in which many people are contributing to the fulfillment of organizational purposes. Conversely, persons may hold an office but exercise it in ways that fail to advance organizational directions. Clearly, constituents expect that persons in an office such as bishop will exercise leadership in fulfilling their responsibilities, which presumably means exhibiting assertive and energetic ways of moving the organization forward.

The office of bishop is established in the constitution of the UMC and protected from any facile change or dissolution (chapter 4 will explore episcopal polity further). The constitution grants broad authority to the office for "the general oversight and promotion of the temporal and spiritual interests of the entire Church" (¶ 45) and for "residential and presidential supervision" of the conferences (¶ 47), including appointment of "ministers to the charges" (¶ 52). Legislative paragraphs empower the office to ordain, to organize missions, to form districts and to appoint district superintendents, to transfer clergy from one conference to another, and a few other specific duties (¶¶ 414-16).

Most of the "specific responsibilities of bishops" listed in the *Discipline*, however, are much less definite and much more a matter of discretion and judgment. Bishops are charged "to teach and uphold the theological traditions of The United Methodist Church" and "to promote and support the evangelistic witness of the whole Church" (¶ 414.5, 7). They are "to provide general oversight for the fiscal and program operations of the annual conference" (¶ 415.2). But exactly in what forms a bishop fulfills these responsibilities is her or his to decide.

While bishops have wide visibility and influence in the Church, and are asked to weigh in on many matters, in fact the *Discipline* gives them little decisive authority beyond making and fixing the appointments. Even their constitutional power to make decisions of church law when presiding over a conference is subject to review by the Judicial Council (¶ 49). Bishops propose no legislation, participate in no conference debates, and have no vote anywhere except in their own Council. They do not decide on the candidacy qualifications even of the people they are asked to ordain.

Yet UM people regularly attribute enormous power to them. Many clergy and laity refer regularly to the "Church hierarchy" and "insist on labeling the bishop as authoritarian because [of] their preconceived understandings of the role," as Smith's study puts it. Some bishops in every era have known how to accumulate power and assure that no major decision is made without them. But many would like to get out of the "hierarchical box" the community puts them in. These bishops surely puzzle over the persistence of hierarchy as a mental framework of Church constituents.[20]

Surveying common attitudes of laity and clergy toward bishops, one might conclude with a recent study by a business professor that people "take comfort from" hierarchies. Even though people fuss and fume about them, hierarchical organizations "help us define ourselves . . . add structure and regularity to our lives [and] give us routines, duties, and responsibilities." Despite all the movements toward leveling pyramids by increasing participation and emphasizing flexible task groups over bureaucratic offices and committees, "hierarchies thrive" in business and in other institutions like the Church.[21] And a hierarchy needs an office at the top—even if, as in the UMC, the office of bishop is clearly not structured as a top-down locus of authority.

Bishops have to be even more concerned, then, with how to use the Church's polity to ensure that power is flowing freely through the organization. In her study of power and leadership in the churches, Martha Ellen Stortz builds on the insight of French philosopher Michel Foucault that power circulates in a community or organization. It is not a scarce commodity to be hoarded. It is a dynamic ("power" in Greek is *dynamis*) that flows depending on many circumstantial and social forces.[22]

Rather than seeing power as statically residing in their office, then, bishops can use their power to *empower* others—making sure that the principles and rules of inclusiveness and participation mandated by Church polity are actually carried through, for example, or publicly recognizing the voices and actions of people previously ignored or marginalized. The more a bishop can enable the people under her care to realize and fulfill their abilities and resources, the more the bishop can actually sponsor the generating of power in the community.

Conclusion

Systemic analysis and interpretation of the Church, whether cultural, relational, productive, political, or another framework, is essential to the practice of episcopacy. All four frameworks discussed here are valid, if partial, ways of understanding the Church as an organization and the role of bishops within it. The cultural frame emphasizes the nature of the Church as a continuing tradition expressed in forms and practices that accrue over time. The relational frame prizes the Church as a communal fellowship. The productive frame asks what impact the Church is having and what it has to show for its work. The political frame addresses the uses of power and arrangements of governance in a complex association. Various constituencies in the Church may value one of these views more than another. Each participant may see the Church differently at different times—in one circumstance mainly as a tradition, in another context primarily as a family, and so on.

Whatever the framework, a systemic view encourages episcopal leaders to see the Church as a dynamic in constant movement, not as static or fixed. It draws the bishops toward continual focus on the interaction of the church system with its surrounding environment of human communities, institutions, and landscapes. It reinforces the biblical wisdom that the ministry of love and justice in Jesus' name is intended for the world and is carried out in homes, neighborhoods, and market squares. What goes on "in church"—inside the system—is preparation for that ministry.

Awareness of the forces and flows of church systems heightens the possibility of bishops acting as they are uniquely positioned to do. From their perspective of systemic oversight, they may be able to identify the singular act or gesture that can turn the system in a more constructive direction. They can give the community language to name its strengths and hopes, and help it define the situations to which it must respond. They can nurture the system away from a defensive posture of seeing its resources as scarce commodities, to an outlook of abundance that calls out unrealized gifts and possibilities and generates new powers and capacities.

Bishops do hold a unique position in the Church's systems. Charged with oversight of the whole Church, they have the possibility of seeing the whole picture with its interactive parts, of grasping the whole movement in its global manifestations. Their *episkopos*, seeing over the whole scope of the Church's ministry and mission, is the heart of the episcopal office and the most profound reason that the Church needs this role. Such a systemic role is given its content and character only through the substance of a particular tradition, however. To the nature of the episcopal office in Methodist traditions we now turn.

Notes

1. See, for example, Part IV of the study authorized by the 1960 General Conference and the Co-ordinating Council, authored by Murray H. Leiffer, *The Episcopacy in the Present Day* (Evanston: Bureau of Social and Religious Research, 1963).

2. Roy H. Short, *The Episcopal Leadership Role in United Methodism* (Nashville: Abingdon Press, 1985).

3. Andy Langford and William H. Willimon, *A New Connection: Reforming The United Methodist Church* (Nashville: Abingdon Press, 1995), p. 93.

4. Shari Caudron, "Where Have All the Leaders Gone?" *Workforce* 81, no. 13 (December 2002): 28-33.

5. Among the numerous books recently published on Welch, see his autobiography, Jack (John Francis) Welch, with John A. Byrne, *Jack: Straight from the Gut* (New York: Warner Business Books, 2001), and Janet Lowe, *Welch: An American Icon* (New York: Wiley, 2001).

6. See Rudolph W. Giuliani, with Ken Kurson, *Leadership* (New York: Hyperion, 2002); Oren Harari, *The Leadership Secrets of Colin Powell* (New York: McGraw-Hill, 2002); and Vince Lombardi Jr., *What It Takes to Be Number 1: Vince Lombardi on Leadership* (New York: McGraw-Hill, 2001).

7. Kenneth H. Blanchard, Bill Hybels, and Phil Hodges, *Leading by the Book: Tools to Transform Your Workspace* (New York: William Morrow, 1999); Laurie Beth Jones, *Jesus CEO: Using Ancient Wisdom for Visionary Leadership* (New York: Hyperion, 1995).

8. Rakesh Khurana, *Searching for a Corporate Savior: The Irrational Quest for Charismatic CEOs* (Princeton: Princeton University Press, 2002), pp. x, 23, and chapter 2; and Judith E. Smith, "What Style of Leadership Will Our Bishops Embody and Model?" in Russell E. Richey, William B. Lawrence, and Dennis M. Campbell, eds., *Questions for the Twenty-first Century Church* (Nashville: Abingdon Press, 1999), pp. 194-215. Quotation from p. 207.

9. For the classic statement of "servant leadership" (written by a corporate CEO and practicing Quaker), see Robert K. Greenleaf, *Servant Leadership: A Journey into the Nature of Legitimate Power and Greatness* (New York: Paulist Press, 1977).

10. Shirley J. Roels, "Organization Man, Organization Woman: Faith, Gender, and Management" in Shirley J. Roels, with Barbara Hilkert Andolsen and Paul F. Camenisch, *Organization Man, Organization Woman: Calling, Leadership, and Culture* (Nashville: Abingdon Press, 1997), pp. 17-79.

11. Roger Friedland and Robert R. Alford, "Bringing Society Back In: Symbols, Practices, and Institutional Contradictions" in Walter W. Powell and Paul J. DiMaggio, eds., *The New Institutionalism in Organizational Analysis* (Chicago: University of Chicago Press, 1991), pp. 232-63. Quotation from p. 248.

12. On secondary logics in religious organizations, see Harry S. Stout and D. Scott Cormode, "Institutions and the Story of American Religion" in N. J. Demerath III, Peter Dobkin Hall, Terry Schmitt, and Rhys H. Williams, eds., *Sacred Companies: Organizational Aspects of Religion and Religious Aspects of Organizations* (New York: Oxford University Press, 1998), pp. 62-78.

13. Langford and Willimon, *New Connection*, pp. 98-99.

14. For further discussion of the burgeoning literature on leadership and its implications for the church, see Thomas Edward Frank, "The Discourse of Leadership and the Practice of Administration," *Journal of Religious Leadership* 1, no. 1 (Spring 2002): 1-15. Online at www.christianleaders.org.

15. Smith, "What Style of Leadership," pp. 199-200.

16. On organizational culture and the church, see Thomas Edward Frank, *The Soul of the Congregation: An Invitation to Congregational Reflection* (Nashville: Abingdon Press, 2000); Carl S. Dudley and Sally A. Johnson, *Energizing the Congregation: Images That*

Shape Your Congregation's Ministry (Louisville: Westminster/John Knox Press, 1993); and James F. Hopewell, *Congregation: Stories and Structures*, ed. Barbara G. Wheeler (Philadelphia: Fortress Press, 1987).

17. Among the many books on the churches as family-like systems, see Charles H. Cosgrove and Dennis D. Hatfield, *Church Conflict* (Nashville: Abingdon Press, 1994); and the classic by Edwin H. Friedman, *Generation to Generation: Family Process in Church and Synagogue* (New York: Guilford Press, 1985).

18. A classic summary of ego psychology may be found in Gertrude and Rubin Black, *Ego Psychology: Theory and Practice* (New York: Columbia University Press, 1974), esp. p. 27 on the organizing and adapting functions of the ego in changing environments.

19. The distinction is pervasive in the literature; see for example, Lovett H. Weems, *Church Leadership* (Nashville: Abingdon Press, 1993), and Smith, "What Style of Leadership," p. 195.

20. Smith, "What Style of Leadership," pp. 202, 206.

21. Harold J. Leavitt, "Why Hierarchies Thrive," *Harvard Business Review* (March 2003): 96-102. Quotations from p. 101.

22. Martha Ellen Stortz, *Pastorpower* (Nashville: Abingdon Press, 1993), p. 24.

Episcopacy in Methodism

Shadows of John Wesley

Nothing has been introduced into Methodism by the present episcopal form of government, which was not before fully exercised by Mr. Wesley.

This claim, advanced by Bishops Coke and Asbury in their 1798 annotated *Discipline*, will doubtless be greeted by most readers, certainly most United Methodists, as self-evident.[1] Of course, Methodist episcopacy continued the leadership style and sustained the prerogatives exercised by Wesley.[2] This, one of the earliest ecclesial claims Methodists have made about themselves, continues to the present as an essential affirmation in Methodist self-understanding and conceptions of mission, ministry, and leadership.[3] What else would one say? How else might it have been? Of course, episcopacy tracks Wesley. But is it so obvious? Should it have been so in early Methodism? Was the Wesleyan style the only one available? Might other models for episcopacy have been viable? Were others even thinkable, visible?

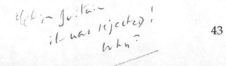

43

What implications followed? What difference has it made that Methodism over the course of its life followed the Wesleyan paradigm? What implications follow for us today? How might our experience with episcopacy shape our ecumenical conversations in our dialogues, with Roman Catholics, with Lutherans, with Episcopalians, and with other Methodists (the Pan-Methodist conversations especially)? And how might this paradigm affect our reaction to current proposals for a four-year presidency in The United Methodist Council of Bishops?

This essay reminds us that Methodist episcopacy is indeed distinctive.[4] What is the norm? Outside of Methodism, in the longer tradition of the church, bishops are not itinerant, general superintendents but diocesan, the keystone to located, diocesan orders.[5]

No Episcopacy: A Prospectus?

When the preachers were hailed together for the Christmas Conference in 1784, they doubtless convened expecting some ecclesial deliverance from John Wesley, some church order with his imprimatur. Their expectations and concerns, at least as we discern them, focused less on a grand ecclesial design than on the day-to-day problems presented by serving a movement lacking access to sacraments and ordination. And, insofar as they had hinted at interests in an ecclesial design, they had shown a predilection for something other than episcopacy.

The regular conference for 1779, just five years prior, had, in the absence of Francis Asbury, taken the matters of sacrament and order into their own hands. They pronounced the "Episcopal Establishment" dissolved, recognized that they existed in an ecclesial vacuum "without the ordinances," constituted a presbytery, empowered that body to ordain and exercise *episkopē*, and issued protocols about the sacraments.[6] This presbyterian church order, we should note, did not summarily break with Wesleyan ministerial patterns. To the contrary it self-consciously preserved the Methodist evangelistic machinery. It explicitly named and continued the array of Wesleyan offices—assistant, preachers, local preachers, exhorters, stewards, trustees. It did so within a nonepiscopal, indeed, a presbyterian framework. And that conference had apparently felt sufficiently confident of its own ecclesial sensibilities and discretion as to preserve some elements of the Anglican order while jettisoning its overall framework. Most significantly, it permitted the use of elements of the communion service from the *Book of Common Prayer* [BCP] in this otherwise nonepiscopal endeavor.

This ecclesial declaration of independence produced schism. Asbury and preachers loyal to him rejected the separation from the Church, preferred to wait for a dispensation from Wesley, refrained from administering the sacraments, and recognized Wesley-like authority in Asbury. Their nod toward authority and pledge not to separate at that point gave some indication of the ecclesial sensitivities of the Asbury loyalists. However, we should note, the Asbury loyalists complained specifically not about the "presbyterial" order that had been adopted but rather about the schismatic and ecclesially problematic self-ordinations and sacramental self-authorizations.[7] Neither the schism nor its healing the following year gave any clear signals about Methodist aspirations for church order. The American Methodists had not made up their ecclesiological mind yet.

By 1784 when the Christmas Conference convened, minus significant portions of their leadership who fled during the Revolution, keenly aware of the massive disarray in what was left of Anglicanism, with reordering and reorganization proceeding in the states and the nation, they might well have been open to various ecclesiastical, structural orders. Not schooled in formal ecclesiologies, nor informed about the evolution of polities, the preachers had nevertheless traveled the colonial landscape, heard its confessional polyphony or cacophony, preached in churches and meeting houses loaned for that purpose and encountered leaders from other traditions. And they were not without guidance on bishops and the norm for episcopal organization. The following experience with episcopal ordering or models might have been instructive either at the 1784 gathering or soon thereafter:

1. That exercised by the Church of England, as perceived in the colonies;
2. That actually established by the Protestant Episcopal Church;
3. That taught by the authorities to whom John Wesley and Thomas Coke appealed in making provision for Methodist polity;
4. That referenced in Coke's sermon and espoused in the service of ordination.

Methodism chose to follow none of these but instead marked its own episcopal path. Its conception of episcopacy is well-known and well-documented and can be seen virtually everywhere in early Methodism. Its episcopal self-understanding we will only nod at as indicated:

1. That explicit or implicit in the first *Disciplines*;
2. That taught in the annotated *Discipline* of 1798;

and in the following chapter—

3. That modeled in Asbury's practice;
4. That found in subsequent episcopal patterns.

In this chapter, then, we offer a counterfactual enquiry, an exploration of episcopal patterns to which the colonial Methodists would have had exposure and that they might have entertained. Against that backdrop the Wesleyan model of episcopacy, what we eventually codify as "itinerant general superintendency" becomes all the more remarkable.

Episcopacy Exercised by the Church of England, as Perceived in the Colonies

The Church of England in the colonies functioned without a resident bishop, its ecclesiastical needs being served from abroad by the bishop of London. However, the colonists could not be said to be lacking ideas about an American bishop or American bishops. Indeed, in just the period when Methodists began their informal work along the eastern seaboard, during the 1760s, proposals for an American episcopate rocked the colonies. Indeed, some historians have argued that the threat of an Anglican episcopate in North America fed the hysteria about English tyranny and constituted one of the grievances that brought on revolution.[8]

The idea of bishops for America, even in colonies, would not seem far-fetched today and the inconvenience of its absence obvious. Bishops are essential for the Church to be the Church and for the Church to do its work. Bishops constitute the fundamental order, office, and unit of the Church. From the episcopal office derive parishes and clergy. From it devolves sacraments and orders (ordinations). From it comes Church membership (through confirmation). Parishioners belong to the bishop's extended congregation. Clergy represent the bishop when he is not present.

But here was an Episcopal Church lacking episcopal presence and leadership. The colonial Anglicans received no transatlantic visits from the bishop within whose trans-Atlantic diocese the colonies lay, though he did send commissaries who could act in his stead for some functions. Not among the commissary's offices were either confirmation or ordination, both fairly essential, the one providing entry into the Church, the other into orders. Young Anglicans could hardly be expected to travel to London to be confirmed. Candidates for orders did so routinely but at great inconvenience and at some risk. One fifth of those sent from New England for ordination died in the cause.

Anglican laity who had grown up in the colonies, particularly in the South where the Church was well-established, seem to have accustomed themselves to a church without bishops. Indeed some southern Anglicans opposed the creation of an American or colonial episcopal office when serious proposals for colonial bishops surfaced. However, an invigorated Anglicanism in the North, led by zealous converts from Puritanism and by a more active Society for the Propagation of the Gospel, thought otherwise. These courageous spirits sought a bishop for the colonies.[9] They did so in the face of deep-seated Calvinist—Puritan and Presbyterian—hostility to bishops and virtual paranoia about what an American episcopate augured for the exercise of English authority in colonial society. To Scottish Presbyterians and New England Puritans bishops were but lackeys of the crown, another scheme or stratagem for imposing the royal will in the colonies.

The proposal for an American Episcopate, advanced by Thomas B. Chandler in a 1767 publication, *An Appeal to the Public*, had been matured in a convocation of Anglican clergy in Elizabeth Town in October 1766, attended by Samuel Johnson, former president of King's College, future Bishop Samuel Seabury, and most of the prominent northern clergy. Behind it lay also secret correspondence between Johnson and Thomas Secker, archbishop of Canterbury. Supporting it publicly abroad was Bishop Joseph Butler and politicking for it was the bishop of London, Thomas Sherlock, who pressured Parliament by cutting back on commissaries. Resisting the idea and doing so vehemently were the leaders in the Reformed communions, including Congregationalists Charles Chauncy and Jonathan Mayhew in Massachuesetts and Presbyterians William Livingston and Francis Alison in New York, the former in pamphlets, the latter in the paper, the *American Whig*.[10] Colonial opponents elicited zealous advocacy against the proposal from the Protestant Dissenters in England who exercised lobbying strength in Parliament far in excess of their numbers. In both the colonies and Parliament, opponents succeeded in labeling the proposal as ecclesiastical tyranny, a threat to Protestant liberties, a political imposition, so concedes the historian of colonial Anglicanism, John Woolverton.[11]

The details of the actual plan, sometimes known as the "Bishop Butler Proposal," need not concern us here, except to note that the colonial crisis and intra-Anglican colonial exchanges about bishops: focused attention on bishops and their role in church and society; opened a debate within and beyond the Anglican Church as to whether the ecclesial functions could be exercised apart from the political role of bishops; occasioned controversy about the relation of bishops to kings; and predisposed the Loyalists who would organize the Protestant Episcopal Church for nonpolitical episcopacy and for suffrage in selection of bishops. The controversy made the reading public aware of bishops and the issue of residence. Of these exchanges about episcopacy and its diocesan nature, one can assume that some, if not all, of the Methodist preachers would have had awareness. After all, as leaders they were expected and pledged themselves—until 1784—to model and to exhort adherence to the Church of England and to take communion regularly from its clergy. And one can certainly wonder whether this controversy informed, to some degree, Asbury's insistence on election to the office.

The Episcopacy Actually Established by/for the Protestant Episcopal Church

Very soon after Methodists put the foundations down for their new episcopal order and as they were beginning its scaffolding, the Anglicans [Episcopalians] began their polity construction. We have little reason to believe that Methodists took an interest in these proceedings. Indeed, Methodists might have behaved differently, left much more detailed minutes, clarified matters of power and authority, and avoided some future trauma and division, had they observed the Episcopalians in convention or even taken a close look at their published proceedings. The Episcopalians showed, from the very start, a much higher degree of constitutional and theological sophistication. That should hardly surprise anyone, as it was Episcopalians authoring the Federal constitution as well as that for a new church.

We should not lose sight, however, of the fact that persons who had been involved in the Methodist movement—folks like Samuel Magaw, Joseph Pilmore, and Devereux Jarratt—remained in the Church. Nor can we ignore the informal conversation that Thomas Coke and Francis Asbury had with Anglican clergy John Andrews and William West in 1784 aimed at forestalling separation, or the secret negotiations that Bishop Thomas Coke carried on with Bishop William White only six years later, negotiations aimed at reuniting Methodists and Episcopalians. The latter conversations included a secret letter sent to White in 1791 in which Coke asserted:

> I am not sure but I went further in the separation of our Church in America, than Mr. Wesley from whom I had received my commission did intend. He did indeed solemnly invest me, as far as he had a right so to do, with Episcopal Authority, but did not intend, I think, that an entire separation should take place. He, being pressed by our friends on this side the water for ministers to administer the sacraments to them, (there being very few Clergy of the Church of England then in the states) went farther I am sure than he would have gone if he had foreseen some events which followed. And this I am certain of—that he is now sorry for the separation.[12]

In outlining issues attendant upon possible reunion, Coke focused in this letter on the matter of the sacraments and whether Methodist preachers would assent to reordination. In another letter, to Bishop Samuel Seabury, he touched on consecration of himself and Asbury as Episcopal bishops. White responded favorably in letter and had several conversations with Coke. Seabury did not respond. Coke's letter and White's response, when uncovered and published a decade later, embarrassed and scandalized Coke.[13]

Important for our considerations in this strange affair is the comfort level that some Methodists showed with the form of episcopacy emerging within the Protestant Episcopal Church. It was thoroughly diocesan, though adjusted to the democratic republican ethos of the new country, "bishops by ballot" as Frederick Mills put it.

From the first Convention, that of 1785, these Anglicans made clear that bishops were essential to the Church. The first "Canon" of the Protestant Episcopal Church conceived of the Church as constituted by its threefold ministry: "In this church there shall always be three orders in the ministry, viz. Bishops, Priests and Deacons." They were equally clear about the diocesan, local nature of bishops. The "General Ecclesiastical Constitution," as crafted by the Convention of 1785, provided that "[E]very Bishop of this Church shall confine the exercise of his Episcopal office to his proper jurisdiction; unless requested to ordain or confirm by an church destitute of a Bishop." When revised in 1789 as Article 4 of "A General Constitution" this provision read: "And every Bishop of this Church shall confine the exercise of his Episcopal office to his proper Diocese or District, unless requested to ordain or confirm, or perform any other act of the Episcopal office, by an church destitute of a Bishop."

Article 7 stipulated that "No person shall be admitted to holy orders, until he shall have been examined by the Bishop, and by two Presbyters."

Canon 3 specified that "Every Bishop in this church shall, as often as may be convenient, visit the churches within his diocese or district, for the purpose of examining the state of his church, inspecting the behaviour of the clergy, and administering the apostolic act of confirmation."

Article 3 provided for a House of Bishops: "The Bishops, when there shall be three or more, shall, whenever General Conventions are held, form a separate House, with a right to originate and propose acts for the concurrence of the House of Deputies." The article went on to care for an Episcopal "negative" on initiatives by the Deputies, unless overridden by a four-fifths majority and to specify that "all acts of the Convention shall be authenticated by both Houses." Article 6 provided for trials of clergy and of bishops.[14] Here, then, was *episkopē*, a version of the established Church that Wesley loved, that preserved its diocesan nature.

Episcopacy as Taught by the Authorities to Whom John Wesley and Thomas Coke Appealed in Making Provision for Methodist Polity

In his authorizing letter "To Dr. Coke, Mr. Asbury, and our Brethren in North America," John Wesley enjoined the Americans to exercise "full liberty, simply to follow the Scriptures and the Primitive Church." Earlier in that missive, Wesley cited the authority for such guidance, one on whom he several times indicated dependence, namely "Lord King's *Account of the Primitive Church*."[15]

Lord Peter King's An *Inquiry into the Constitution, Discipline, Unity, and Worship of the Primitive Church* figured prominently in Methodist apologetics from John Wesley onward. It presented, however, an estimate and understanding of episcopacy that differed radically from that which unfolded in the new church. King sounded from the start a recurrent theme "but one bishop, strictly so called, in a church at a time, who was related to his flock as a pastor to his sheep, and a parent to his children." And further "there was but one church to a bishop . . . the ancient dioceses are never said to contain churches, in the plural, but only a church, in the singular." He continued, "the bishops' dioceses exceeded not the bounds of a modern parish" and the "bishop had but one altar or communion table in his whole diocese."[16] The work of the bishop,

> the peculiar acts of his function were such as these: viz., preaching the word, praying with his people, administering the two sacraments of baptism, and the Lord's supper, taking care of the poor, ordaining of ministers, governing his flock, excommunicating of offenders, absolving of penitents; and, in a word, whatever acts can be comprised under those three general heads of preaching, worship, and government, were part of the bishop's function and office.[17]

These located, pastoral officers, "the primitive apostolic bishops," he continued, "constantly resided with their flocks, conscientiously applying themselves with the utmost diligence and industry, to the promotion of the spiritual welfare of those that were committed to their trust. . . ." And the episcopal election process accorded with this local pattern, selection by the clergy and laity of the parish, thereafter presenting "him to the neighbouring bishops for their approbation and consent, because, without their concurrent assent, there could be no bishop legally instituted or confirmed." The new bishop would then be ordained or installed in "his own church" by neighboring bishops.[18] Only after establishing the nature and work of the bishop did King proceed to the theme that endeared him to Methodist apologists and evoked the Wesley citation, arguing against a continuous historic succession, insisting that bishops were equal to presbyters in order, though superior in degree, and noting instances of presbyterial ordination of bishops.[19]

To Edward Stillingfleet, Methodists also looked for their understanding of polity and episcopacy, as John wrote to Charles in 1780:

> Dear Brother—Read Bishop Stillingfleet's *Irenicon* or any impartial history of the Ancient church, and I believe you will think as I do. I verily believe I have as good a right to ordain as to administer the Lord's supper.

But I see abundance of reasons why I should not use that right, unless I was turned out of the Church. At present we are just in our place.[20]

Stillingfleet's work bore its soul in the title: *Irenicum; A Weapon Salve for the Church's Wounds; or, The Divine Right of Particular Forms of Church Government, Discussed and Examined according to the Principles of the Law of Nature, the Positive Laws of God, the Practice of the Apostles, and the Primitive Church, and the Judgment of Reformed Divines.* Stillingfleet cited "the learned Is. Casaubon" on the "polity of the primitive church":

> Bishops, together with presbyters, were appointed in each of the churches, and every one, by his singular care, taking charge of his own, and all of the whole in common interest, gave a specimen of a certain kind of admirable aristocracy.

Stillingfleet then proceeded, with great care, to explore the provision for and understanding of polity that could be inferred from the law of nature, explicit commands of the Scripture, appointment by Christ, the practice of the apostles, patterns in the early Church, subsequent ecclesial experience, and the instruction of the Reformers. None of these, he showed, exhibited one pattern, certainly not one that should be accorded "divine right." Instead, he found great diversity of precept and practice, as this summary along the way suggests:

> Our inquiry then is, whether the primitive church did conceive itself obliged to observe unalterably one individual form of government, as delivered down to them either by a law of Christ, or an universal constitution of the apostles; or else did only settle and order things for church government, according as it judged them tend most to the peace and settlement of the church, without any antecedent obligation, as necessarily binding to observe only one course. This latter I shall endeavour to make out to have been the only rule and law which the primitive church observed as to church government, viz. the tendency of its constitutions to the peace and unity of the church; and not any binding law or practice of Christ or his apostles. . . . For, if the power of the church and its officers did increase merely from the enlargement of the bounds of churches; if not one certain form was observed in all churches, but great varieties as to officers and dioceses; if the course used in settling the power of the chief officers of the church was from agreement with the civil government; if, notwithstanding the superiority of bishops, the ordination of presbyters was owned as valid; if in all other things concerning the church's polity, the church's prudence was

looked on as a sufficient ground to establish things; then we may with reason conclude, that nothing can be inferred from the practice of the primitive church, demonstrative of any one fixed form of church government delivered from the apostles to them.[21]

Stillingfleet concluded his 440-page exploration with three words of counsel, "three general principles":

> [P]rudence must be used in settling the government of the church.
> [T]hat form of government is the best according to principles of Christian prudence, which comes the nearest to apostolical practice, and tends most to the advancing the peace and unity of the church of God.
> What form of government is determined by lawful authority in the church of God, ought so far to be submitted to, as it contains nothing repugnant to the Word of God.

In explicating the latter point he pled for "liberty in the church," the exercise of "lawful authority" and the healing of divisions. In explicating the second point, Stillingfleet offered his reading of what "were unquestionably of the primitive practice."

> Such are the restoring of the presbyteries of several churches, as the senate to the bishop, with whose counsel and advice all things were done in the primitive church. The contracting of dioceses into such a compass as may be fitted for the personal inspection of the bishop, and care of himself and the senate; the placing of bishops in all great towns of resort, especially county towns; that according to the ancient course of the church, its government may be proportioned to the civil government. The constant preaching of the bishop in some churches of his charge, and residence in his dioceses; the solemnity of ordinations, with the consent of the people; the observing provincial synods twice every year. The employing of none in judging church matters but the clergy. These are things unquestionably of the primitive practice, and no argument can be drawn from the present state of things, why they are not as much, if not more necessary than ever. And therefore all who appeal to the practice of the primitive church, must condemn themselves, if they justify the neglect of them.[22]

To King and Stillingfleet the Methodists might and did look for counsel and theological armament in defending their episcopacy. Following their model of episcopacy they did not.

Episcopacy as Preached and Celebrated in the Ordination of Asbury

There should be really no confusion about character of church or leadership formed in 1784. It was episcopal.[23] The first *Discipline* proclaimed, "We will form ourselves into an Episcopal Church under the Direction of Superintendents, Elders, Deacons and Helpers, according to the Forms of Ordination annexed to our Liturgy, and the Form of Discipline set forth in these Minutes."[24] The name given to the Church was Methodist *Episcopal*. The Church established the threefold ministerial offices. It termed that office most responsible for *episkopē* "superintendent" and used that term consistently through the ordination service. It was, however, an "ordination" and the service employed was that for the Anglican order of bishops, abridged slightly in the characteristic Wesleyan fashion and with that consistent terminological shift.[25] Coke preached an ordination sermon, one major portion of which delineated "the character of a Christian bishop." He defended Methodist ordinations, those by Wesley and those in which he was taking a hand, drawing on such authorities as King and Stillingfleet. He represented the exercise of this office as "episcopal," insisting:

> [W]e have every qualification for an episcopal church which that of Alexandria (a church of no small note in the primitive times) possessed for two hundred years. Our bishops, or superintendents (as we rather call them,) having been elected or received by the suffrages of the whole body of our ministers through the continent, assembled in general conference.

Coke appealed to authorities to argue against the existence of an unbroken apostolic succession, in parts of the Church where episcopacy was sustained. He explicitly affirmed Methodism to be creating an episcopal polity.

> But of all the forms of church government, we think a *moderate* episcopacy the best. The executive power being lodged in the hands of one, or at least a few, vigor and activity are given to the resolves of the body, and those two essential requisites for any grand undertaking are sweetly united—calmness and wisdom in deliberating; and in the executive department, expedition and force.

Coke then proceeded to "consider the grand characteristics of a Christian bishop," ten traits, be it remembered, he identified as he prepared to "ordain" Mr. Asbury. They included humility, meekness, gentleness, patience, fortitude, impartiality, zeal, wisdom, communion with God and confidence in God, and seriousness. Coke elaborated on each virtue. Both the list of traits and their elaboration suggested a fairly traditional, diocesan, view of the office. For instance, of "his *impartiality*" Coke affirmed:

> This is the rarest of all the virtues, and yet one of the most important for a ruler of the church. There is nothing more intolerable to mankind than partiality in him that governs; and it always springs in part from a meanness and baseness of mind. It meets with such immediate and effectual resistance, that all the reins of discipline are dropped, and the vineyard of the Lord thrown open to every beast of prey. . . .[26]

Such homiletical counsel might suggest that Coke envisioned and the members of the Christmas Conference could anticipate an episcopacy whose locale was diocesan, whose style was pastoral, whose work was sacramental, and whose administration was provincial. If so, they were to be profoundly disappointed.

Methodist episcopacy would not follow the patterns of Anglicanism. It would not take cues from the colonial crisis over bishops; nor learn from protocols for episcopacy of the emerging Protestant Episcopal Church. It would not adhere to the counsel of the authorities on whom Wesley, Coke, and early Methodists legitimated their orders; nor would it listen attentively to Coke. Instead, American Methodists would follow the scriptural *episkopos* model scripted by John Wesley, a missional conception achieving its teaching tasks and its responsibilities for the oneness, holiness, catholicity, and apostolicity of the Church in distinctively Wesleyan fashion.[27]

Episcopacy as Explicit or Implicit in the First *Discipline*

The legislation in the first *Discipline* deserves citation in full for the succinct, indeed terse, way in which it outlined a Wesleyan conception of the episcopal office:

> Q. 2. What can be done in order to the future Union of the Methodists?

A. During the life of Rev. Mr. Wesley, we acknowledge ourselves his Sons in the Gospel, ready in Matters belonging to Church-Government, to obey his Commands. And we do engage after his Death, to do every Thing that we judge consistent with the Cause of Religion in America and the political Interests of these States, to preserve and promote our Union with the Methodists in Europe.

Q. 3. As the Ecclesiastical as well as Civil Affairs of these United States have passed through a very considerable Change by the Revolution, what Plan of Church-Government shall we hereafter pursue?

A. We will form ourselves into an Episcopal Church under the Direction of Superintendents, Elders, Deacons and Helpers [lay preachers], according to the Forms of Ordination annexed to our Liturgy, and the Form of Discipline set forth in these Minutes.

Q. 26. What is the Office of a Superintendent?

A. To ordain *Superintendents, Elders,* and *Deacons;* to preside as a Moderator in our Conferences; to fix the Appointments of the Preachers for the several Circuits: and in the Intervals of the Conference, to change, receive or suspend Preachers, as Necessity may require; and to receive Appeals from the Preachers and People, and decide them.

N. B. No Person shall be ordained a Superintendent, Elder or Deacon, without the Consent of a Majority of the Conference and the Consent and Imposition of Hands of a Superintendent; except in the Instance provided for in the 29th Minute.

Q. 27. To whom is the Superintendent amenable for his Conduct?

A. To the Conference: who have Power to expel him for improper Conduct, if they see necessary.

Q. 28. If the Superintendent ceases from Travelling at large among the People, shall he still exercise his Office in any Degree?

A. If he ceases from Travelling without the Consent of the Conference, he shall not thereafter exercise any ministerial Function whatsoever in our Church.

Q. 29. If by Death, Expulsion or otherwise there be no Superintendents remaining in our Church, what shall we do?

A. The Conference shall elect a Superintendent, and the Elders or any three of them shall ordain him according to our Liturgy.[28]

The office of superintendent or bishop traced the work and style of John Wesley, and Question 28 punctuated that dependence dramatically. The

American Methodist commitment to Wesley has often and appropriately elicited comment on the relation of the new church to Wesley, on how and whether his authority continued, and on his and their intentions for the principals concerned:

> During the life of Rev. Mr. Wesley, we acknowledge ourselves his Sons in the Gospel, ready in Matters belonging to Church-Government, to obey his Commands.

This commitment bears as well on the nature of the episcopal office in the new church. It might be read not only as continuing Wesley's exercise of *episkopē*, but also as sustaining the kind of *episkopē* that Wesley exercised.

Methodists have devoted considerable attention from 1784 on to the names bestowed on the office—superintendent and bishop—and to the implications that follow from accenting the one or the other. Names do signify. Names do legitimate. Names do empower. Not surprisingly, debates over the name employed for and the authority and power of our itinerant, general superintendents figure prominently in Methodist squabbles thereafter and in most of the schisms of the movement.

In 1787, the bishops (and apparently it was Asbury) altered the *Doctrines and Discipline*, substituting the term "bishop" for that of "superintendent." According to Jesse Lee, Asbury made the substitution first and asked the next conference to ratify the change as the scriptural name and equivalent in meaning.[29] This change prompted the severe scolding from John Wesley and the lyrical parody from Charles.

Asbury nevertheless had no difficulty in applying either "bishop" or "superintendent" to himself and fellow bishops and used the terms as interchangeable and synonymous, so argues Spellmann.[30]

Episcopacy as Taught by the Bishops in Their Annotated *Discipline* of 1798

At the directive of the General Conference of 1796, Bishops Coke and Asbury undertook an annotation of, commentary upon, or exegesis of the *Discipline*. Precipitating this remarkable exercise of *episkopē* were the revolt of James O'Kelly and his scathing attack on the nature and exercise of Methodist authority. The Bishops naturally gave special attention to matters criticized—the legitimacy of Methodist order and orders, itinerancy, discipline, the presiding eldership and episcopacy. One of their longest statements, not surprisingly, given O'Kelly's attack on the office, Section IV, "Of the Election and Consecration of Bishops, and of their Duty,"[31] devoted seven pages of very fine type to the short disciplinary delineation of Methodist episcopacy. They begin the exposition with the statement that heads this chapter:

> In considering the present subject, we must observe that nothing has been introduced into Methodism by the present episcopal form of government, which was not before fully exercised by Mr. Wesley. He presided in the conferences; fixed the appointments of the preachers for their several circuits; changed, received, or suspended preachers, wherever he judged that necessity required it; travelled through the European connection at large; superintended the spiritual and temporal business; and consecrated two bishops, Thomas Coke and Alexander Mather, one before the present episcopal plan took place in America, and the other afterwards, besides ordaining elders and deacons. But the authority of Mr. Wesley and that of the bishops in America differ in . . . important points. . . .

The bishops claimed the several dimensions of Wesley's *episkopē*, but then contrasted their authority with that of Mr. Wesley, suggesting in effect that his "general" and "superintending" powers quite exceeded theirs, points to which we return in the following chapter. They were clear, however, that Wesleylike itinerancy, particularly their itinerancy and their appointment of preachers out of their circulation through the entirety of the Methodist work, connected and united the movement.

> *Our grand plan*, in all its parts, leads to an *itinerant* ministry. Our bishops are *travelling* bishops. All the different orders which compose our conferences are employed in the *travelling line*; and our local preachers are, *in some degree*, travelling preachers. Everything is kept moving as far as possible; and we will be bold to say, that, next to the grace of God, there is nothing *like this* for keeping the whole body alive from the centre to the circumference, and for the continual extension of that circumference on every hand.

They knew a church characterized by such itinerancy and bishops so epitomized differed markedly from churches and authority since the days of the apostles.

Where is the like in any other episcopal church? It would be a disgrace to our episcopacy, to have bishops settled on their plantations here and there, evidencing to all the world, that instead of breathing the spirit of their office, they could, without remorse, lay down their crown, and bury the most important talents God has given men! We would rather choose that our episcopacy should be blotted out from the face of the earth, than be spotted with such disgraceful conduct! All the episcopal churches in the world are conscious of the dignity of their episcopal office. The greatest part of the endeavour to preserve this dignity by large salaries, splendid dresses, and other appendages of pomp and splendour. But if an episcopacy has neither the dignity which arises from these worldly trappings, nor that infinitely superior dignity which is the attendant of labour, of suffering and enduring hardship for the cause of Christ, and of a venerable old age, the concluding scene of a life, devoted to the service of God, it instantly becomes the disgrace of a church and the just ridicule of the world!

Bishops Asbury and Coke made clear that itinerancy defined *episkopē*, that it reclaimed the patterns of the apostolic church, and that it functioned to sustain the oneness, holiness, and catholicity of apostolicity:

> We have already quoted . . . many texts of Scripture in defence of episcopacy and the itinerant plan, . . . The whole tenor of St. Paul's epistles to Timothy and Titus clearly evidences, that they were invested, on the whole, with abundantly more power than our bishops: nor does it appear that they were responsible to any but God and the apostle. The text quoted in the notes on the 3rd section, in defence of the itinerant plan, we would particularly recommend to the reader's attention; as we must insist upon it, that the general itinerancy would not probably exist for any length of time on this extensive continent, if the bishops were not invested with that authority which they now possess. They alone travel through the whole connection, and, therefore, have such a view of the whole, as no yearly conference can possibly have.

Itinerancy provided a connectional view, a grasp of the whole, the ability to resist local partialities, passions, and prejudices. Itinerancy made general superintendency possible.

Notes

1. The epigraph is from Thomas Coke and Francis Asbury, *The Doctrines and Disciplines of the Methodist Episcopal Church, in America* (Philadelphia: Henry Tuckniss, 1798), p. 38;

also in Russell E. Richey, Kenneth E. Rowe, and Jean Miller Schmidt, *The Methodist Experience in America: A Sourcebook*, II (Nashville: Abingdon Press, 2000), 1798, p. 123. "Wesley's ministry laid the essential foundation of what became the Methodist style of episcopacy, and in many ways that foundation has remained intact in America," Gerald F. Moede, "Bishops in the Methodist Tradition: Historical Perspectives," in Jack M. Tuell and Roger W. Fjeld, eds., *Episcopacy: Lutheran-United Methodist Dialogue II* (Minneapolis: Augsburg, 1991), pp. 52-69; quote on p. 58. For an overview and assessment of the office, see James E. Kirby, *The Episcopacy in American Methodism* (Nashville: Abingdon Press/Kingswood, 2000); Thomas Edward Frank, *Polity, Practice, and the Mission of The United Methodist Church*, updated edition (Nashville: Abingdon Press, 2002), pp. 229-53; James K. Mathews, *Set Apart to Serve: The Meaning and Role of Episcopacy in the Wesleyan Tradition* (Nashville: Abingdon Press, 1985); and Roy Hunter Short, *Chosen to Be Consecrated: The Bishops of The Methodist Church, 1784–1968* (Lake Junaluska: Commission on Archives and History for the Council of Bishops, 1976).

See also Norman Woods Spellmann, "The General Superintendency in American Methodism, 1784–1870" (Ph.D. diss., Yale University, April 1961). Note his insistence that the converse of the bishops' claim was not entirely true. That is, there were aspects of Wesley's scriptural *episkopē* that American Methodism did not follow, most notably the focusing and centralizing of authority in the office with something like the ruling, determinative, controlling, autocratic power and authority of Mr. Wesley himself:

> According to Wesley's plan, the Methodist Church in America would have been an episcopal Church of the most extreme type, governed wholly by bishops, without an American general conference or legislative body of any sort. The bishops would have governed in America as Wesley did in England, calling the preachers together from time to time to discuss local matters and to receive their appointments; but all legislative and executive powers would have been inherent in the bishops themselves, subject to Wesley during his life, and to the British Conference after his death. (79)

2. Gerald F. Moede, *The Office of Bishop in Methodism: Its History and Development* (Zurich: Publishing House of the Methodist Church; New York and Nashville: Abingdon Press, 1964), p. 51.

3. Mathews, *Set Apart to Serve*, pp. 38, 63.

4. William B. Oden speaks of "a totally new type of bishop never before seen in the church," Mathews and Oden, eds., *Vision and Supervision: A Sourcebook*, p. 558.

5. Kirby, *The Episcopacy in American Methodism*.

6. "Minutes of a Conference Held at Roger Thomson's in Fluvanna County, Va., May 18, 1779," in *The Methodist Experience in America: A Sourcebook*, eds. Russell E. Richey, Kenneth E. Rowe, and Jean Miller Schmidt (Nashville: Abingdon Press, 2000), pp. 63-65. [*The Methodist Experience* hereinafter referenced as MEA.] Published originally in the *Western Christian Advocate* (26 May 1837): 18-19.

7. *Minutes of the Methodist Conferences, Annually Held in America; From 1773 to 1813, Inclusive* (New York: Daniel H. H. and Thomas Ware for the Methodist Connexion in the United States, 1813), 1779, pp. 19-20.

8. The classic studies of this controversy are Arthur L. Cross, *The Anglican Episcopate and the American Colonies* (New York: Longmans, Green and Co., 1902); Carl Bridenbaugh, *Mitre and Sceptre: Transatlantic Faiths, Ideas, Personalities, and Politics,*

1689–1775 (London, Oxford, New York: Oxford University Press, 1962); and Frederick V. Mills Sr., *Bishops by Ballot: An Eighteenth-Century Ecclesiastical Revolution* (New York: Oxford University Press, 1978). See also Nancy Rhoden, *Revolutionary Anglicanism: The Colonial Church of England Clergy During the American Revolution* (New York: New York University Press, 1999) and Peter Doll, *Revolution, Religion and National Identity: Imperial Anglicanism in British North America, 1745–1795* (Madison, N.J.: Fairleigh Dickinson University Press, 2000).

9. David Lynn Holmes, *A Brief History of the Episcopal Church* (Valley Forge, Pa.: Trinity Press International, 1993), pp. 42-46, 48. John Frederick Woolverton, *Colonial Anglicanism in North America* (Detroit: Wayne State University Press, 1984), pp. 81-135, 220-38. Diana Hochstedt Butler, *Standing Against the Whirlwind: Evangelical Episcopalians in Nineteenth-Century America* (New York: Oxford University Press, 1995), pp. 3-9.

10. Robert W. Prichard, *A History of the Episcopal Church* (Harrisburg, Pa.: Morehouse Publishing, 1991), pp. 61-64.

11. Woolverton, *Colonial Anglicanism*, pp. 220-33.

12. MEA, 1791a, p. 103. The letter, White's response, and sources are indicated on pp. 103-6. For discussion of this whole episode, see Thomas B. Neely, *The Evolution of Episcopacy and Organic Methodism* (New York: Phillips and Hunt; Cincinnati: Cranston and Stowe, 1888), pp. 235-73.

13. See Paul F. Blankenship, "Coke-White Correspondence," *The Encyclopedia of World Methodism*, 2 vols., ed. Nolan B. Harmon et al. (Nashville: The United Methodist Publishing House, 1974), I, pp. 532-33.

14. Journal of a Convention 1785, and subsequent sessions produced constitution and canons, the 1789 version of the "Canons" and of "A General Constitution" being regarded as normative. See *Journals of the General Conventions of the Protestant Episcopal Church, in the United States of America; from the year 1784, to the year 1814, Inclusive* (Philadelphia: Printed and published by John Bieren, 1817), pp. 9, 58-60, 61-62, 75-77, 93-99. Compare Jackson A. Dykman and Edwin Augustine White, *Annotated Constitution and Canons for the Government of the Protestant Episcopal Church in the United States of America, Adopted in General Conventions, 1789–1952*, 2d rev. ed., 2 vols. (Greenwich, Conn.: Seabury Press, 1954), I, pp. 40-41, 103, 108.

15. John Telford, ed., *The Letters of the Rev. John Wesley*, 9 vols. (London: Epworth Press, 1931), 7:237-38; also in MEA, 1784a, pp. 71-72.

16. Lord Peter King, *An Inquiry into the Constitution, Discipline, Unity, and Worship of the Primitive Church: That Flourished within the First Three Hundred Years after Christ: Faithfully Collected out of the Extant Writings of those Ages by Peter King, with an introduction by the American editor* (New York: G. Lane and P. P. Sandford for the Methodist Episcopal Church, 1841; originally published in London: J. Robinson and J. Wyat, 1691), pp. 29, 30, 32, 33.

17. Ibid., *Inquiry*, p. 53.

18. Ibid., *Inquiry*, pp. 55-58.

19. Ibid., *Inquiry*, pp. 60-82. On this issue and the other dimensions to the legitimacy of Wesley's action in ordination and therefore of the validity of Methodist orders as a whole and of episcopacy in particular, we do not attend here. For an interesting positive case from an Anglican standpoint, see R. J. Cooke, D.D., *The Historic Episcopate: A Study of Anglican Claims and Methodist Orders* (New York: Phillips and Hunt; Cincinnati: Cranston and Stowe, 1896), his attention to persuasive grounds in appeals to Scripture,

to the practice of the primitive church, and to necessity, pp. 186-202, and his final chapter on "Doctrine of Necessity: Power of the Church," pp. 203-21.

20. Telford, ed., *Letters*, VII, 21. See also the editorial note on that point, pp. 20-21. Also compare his earlier letter to Charles of 1755, III, p. 135. In a letter to James Clark of July 1756, Wesley affirmed, "I still believe 'the Episcopal form of Church government to be both scriptural and apostolical': I mean, well agreeing with the practice and writings of the Apostles. But that it is prescribed in Scripture I do not believe. This opinion (which I once heartily espoused) I have been heartily ashamed of ever since I read Dr. Stillingfleet's *Irenicon*. I think he has unanswerably proved that neither Christ or His Apostles prescribed any particular form of Church government, and that the pleas for the divine right of Episcopacy was never heard of in the primitive Church," III, p. 182. Wesley appealed to Stillingfleet again in a 1761 letter to the Earl of Dartmouth, again citing him in reference to church government, IV, p. 150.

21. Edward Stillingfleet, *Irenicum; A Weapon Salve for the Church's Wounds; or, The Divine Right of Particular Forms of Church Government, Discussed and Examined According to the Principles of the Law of Nature, the Positive Laws of God, the Practice of the Apostles, and the Primitive Church, and the Judgment of Reformed Divines: Whereby a Foundation Is Laid for the Church's Peace, and the Accommodation of Our Present Differences*, 2nd ed., with an appendix concerning the power of excommunication in a Christian church (Philadelphia: M. Sorin, 1842; originally published in 1662), pp. xiv, 370.

22. Stillingfleet, *Irenicum*, pp. 438-41.

23. See Spellmann, *The General Superintendency*, pp. 68-73.

24. For the text of the first *Discipline* in parallel columns with the "Large Minutes" see Jno. J. Tigert, *A Constitutional History of American Episcopal Methodism*, 3rd. ed. (Nashville: Publishing House of the Methodist Episcopal Church, South, 1908), p. 535.

25. See Nolan B. Harmon Jr., *The Rites and Ritual of Episcopal Methodism* (Nashville: Publishing House of the M. E. Church, South, 1926), pp. 378-408, for the parallel columns of the *BCP* and 1784 rituals.

26. Thomas Coke, *Substance of a Sermon Preached at Baltimore, Maryland before The General Conference of The Methodist Episcopal Church, December 27, 1784 at the Ordination of The Rev. Francis Asbury to the Office of a Superintendent* (New York: Published at the desire of the Conference by T. Mason and G. Lane, 1784).

27. Moede, "Bishops in the Methodist Tradition: Historical Perspectives," *Episcopacy*, pp. 52-60.

28. MEA, 1785a, pp. 82-83. *Minutes of Several Conversations Between the Rev. Thomas Coke, LL. D., the Rev. Francis Asbury and Others, at a Conference, Begun in Baltimore, in the State of Maryland, on Monday, the 27th of December, in the Year 1784* (Philadelphia: Charles Cist, 1785), pp. 3-4, 9-20. Excerpts.

29. Jesse Lee, *A Short History of the Methodists* (Baltimore: Magill and Clime, 1810), p. 128.

30. Spellmann, *The General Superintendency*, pp. 96-98.

31. MEA, 1798, pp. 123-31, excerpted from Thomas Coke and Francis Asbury, *The Doctrines and Discipline* (1798), pp. 38-46.

CHAPTER THREE

Itinerant General Superintendency

Asbury's Precept and Practice

T he "doctrine" of episcopacy enshrined in the Restrictive Rules, the "Constitution" of 1808—itinerant general superintendency—did, indeed, draw upon John Wesley's exercise of *episkopē*. However, the Methodist Episcopal version thereof underwent some significant nuancing in the new world. Much of that Francis Asbury drafted or scripted or embodied, more than any other person or agency. And he wrote it as much by his example and activity as by his statements. We might term it an enacted theology, a practical theology dramatized before Methodist eyes, a theology embodied in practice.

A practical or experimental theology Methodists claim and have claimed as characteristically theirs,[1] perhaps adding some acknowledgment that John Wesley was not a systematic theologian, that his overriding concern lay in mapping the scriptural way of salvation and guiding the lost thereon, and that Charles put the essential Wesleyan guidance and landmarks on Methodist lips. Our hymnal, we affirm with Wesley, functioned as "a little body of experimental and practical divinity."[2] So Methodists have been clear that Wesley's theology guided practice, that its concerns produced disciplines to shape piety, that it aimed at holiness. Methodists have been less clear that it worked vice versa. We have been surprisingly reticent to look at our polity and practice as structured or enacted theology, except perhaps for actual performances of piety, including hymnody. We tend not to examine our recurrent practices, habits, and institutions for the theology therein graphed.

Certainly our hesitancy to do such theological explication or translation out of polity in general and episcopacy in particular is understandable. The office elicited controversy from the very start and figured prominently in every crisis or schism thereafter. Our schisms have tended to feature matters of polity and practice not doctrine, with episcopacy as the flashpoint. James O'Kelly put it bluntly: *as in at Britain*

> I only say no man among us ought to get into the Apostle's chair with the Keys, and stretch a lordly power over the ministers and Kingdom of Christ. . . . Boys with their Keys, under the absolute sway of one who declares his authority and succession from the Apostles—these striplings must rule and govern Christ's Church, as master workmen; as though they could finish such a temple. . . . I am a friend to Christ; to his Church, but not to prelatick government.[3] *whew~!*

Against such exaggerated criticism, Methodist apologists did well to defend bishops in their actual exercise of authority and to ground the authority routinely exercised in Wesleyan example and scriptural precept—as Coke and Asbury themselves did in the 1798 *Discipline*. At best, they hinted at a theology of the office. More can and should be said. And such a theology Asbury does indeed articulate and enact.

The Doctrine of Itinerant General Superintendency

One may read Asbury's enactment of *episkopē* best by separating the three rubrics—itinerant, general, superintendent. Each describes activities and practices that capture historic aspects of episcopacy and of ministry. Each conveys important Methodist nuances as well. "Itinerant" may be the trickiest, since on its face, it connotes simply travel. However, as we have already seen, Methodists haul out the Scripture and cite Wesley's example, defending travel with great verve and extraordinary energy and

1/n – but!

remarkable consistency. We will note Asbury's highly self-conscious modeling of itinerancy and suggest that it stands for Wesleyan spirituality or piety and for *sacrament*. "General" we will take to refer to the teaching office, something that Wesley exercised consummately and the Americans did more with than we have been told. It stands for *Word*. "Superintendent" clearly references the appointive power, the care for discipline, the preservation of our connectional system. It stands for *order*.

We Methodists have typically viewed Asbury, as we Americans have construed George Washington, as the father of our enterprise. That can be readily seen in the various treatments of Asbury, beginning with those rendered while he lived or immediately thereafter (especially Ezekiel Cooper's memorial sermon cum biography)[4] and proceeding down to the present. Those statements rightly treat him as the shaper of the Methodist connection, of our episcopacy, of a genuinely national itinerancy, of an American church. As with Washington and Lincoln, we have gotten "right" with Asbury in every period, lifting up aspects of his life and work important for the day. He played many roles, particularly in relation to the preachers—exemplar, guide, mentor, teacher, appointment-maker, disciplinarian, strategist, apostle. His strengths and contributions, many as they were, cohere in his self-understanding and self-reference in traveling.

Given the centrality of this attribute of Methodism—itinerancy—one cannot help being struck by how recurrent a theme it is in Asbury's *Journal* and *Letters*,[5] a sampling of which over the several decades follows:

> I remain in New York, though unsatisfied with our being both in town together. I have not yet the thing which I seek—a circulation of preachers, to avoid partiality and popularity. However, I am fixed to the Methodist plan, and do what I do faithfully as to God. . . .
>
> At present I am dissatisfied. I judge we are to be shut up in the cities this winter. My brethren seem unwilling to leave the cities, but I think I shall show them the way.[6]
>
> I am in peace, and much blest always when travelling.[7]
>
> I have served the church upwards of twenty-five years in Europe and America. All the property I have gained is two old horses, the constant companions of my toil, 6 if not 7,000 miles every year. When we have no ferry-boats, they swim the rivers. . . .
>
> I soar, indeed, but it is over the tops of the highest mountains we have, which may vie with the Alps. I creep sometimes upon my hands and knees up the slippery ascent; and to serve the church, and

the ministers of it, what I gain is many a reflection from both sides of the Atlantic.[8]

Some may think, that the mode of travelling, which the bishops are obliged to pursue, is attended with little difficulty, and much pleasure. Much pleasure they certainly do experience, because they know that they move in the will of God, and that the Lord is pleased to own their feeble labours. But if to travel through the heat and the cold, the rain and the snow, the swamps and the rivers, over mountains and through the wilderness, lying for nights together on the bare ground and in log-houses, open to the wind on every side, fulfilling their appointments, as far as possible, whatever be the hindrance,—if these be little difficulties, then our bishops have but little to endure.[9]

I am paid for the desperate roads and 5000 miles riding this year; but hope it will be 6000 next. Only let me retreat at night and I am ready by grace for duty every day. . . . [10]

On virtually every page of his journal, Asbury comments on his traveling, sometimes in weariness, sometimes in pride, sometimes in exhortation, often in detail and specifics. I rode, I rode, I rode.

Itinerancy as Typology

Asbury's repetitive exhortation to travel and ruminations thereon invite us to probe what might be meant by itinerancy. Three patterns of traveling might be discerned, each rich theologically, biblically, and spiritually. The first and oldest wandering evokes the biblical figure Abraham and the wandering Arameans.[11] Like the ancient Arameans, wanderers have no fixed destination. They tent in one place and then another, making each as much home as possible. They remain nomads, constantly open to the directions from on high. In that openness, preparedness, responsiveness lies their spirituality, garb for the road, relationship to God.

A second kind of traveling is that of *quest*. These travelers flee Pharaoh. They traverse a wilderness, whether of foliage or of technology. Their home lies beyond wilderness—in Canaan. There they expect spiritual fulfillment, commandments fulfilled, free and proper worship of God.

The third kind of traveling is *pilgrimage*. These travelers head, whether periodically or only once, to a sacred site. From thence they return home, spiritually refreshed, covenant renewed. The land traveled through—going or coming—is neither here nor there.

Wandering: A Scriptural Mandate

Francis Asbury wandered the entire connection. However his movement was not aimless, as inspection of his *Journal* will readily show. He followed the preachers as they formed new circuits. He headed toward any quarterly or camp meeting that lay close to his route. He aimed for each of the conferences, scheduled—once they multiplied—so that he could make it from one to the other. His journeys quite literally encompassed the connection. And wherever he found himself, he symbolized the entirety of the connection's interest in that place. His travels possessed a certain openness or freedom, as did that of the preachers on two- or four- or six-week circuits, but preachers appointed for one another and even for the bishop. With the freedom of itinerating went the accountability of appointments. Asbury counseled never to disappoint one.

Such connectionwide travel indeed gave Asbury the wider vision, the view of the whole, the ecumenical perspective that he referenced in frequent statements, as for instance that cited at the end of the last chapter. This catholicity was apostolic:

> We have already shewn, that *Timothy* and *Titus* were *travelling bishops*. In short, every candid person, who is thoroughly acquainted with the New Testament, must allow, that whatever excellencies other plans may have, *this* is the primitive and *apostolic plan.*[12]

Itinerancy, traveling ministry, itinerant general superintendency have become such code words and common places with us that it is difficult for most of us, I would suspect, to recapture the spiritual force latent with them. On that, however, Asbury certainly made an effort. He did so with the images and valuations employed to image traveling and to image its opposite—locality. With the one went positive and scriptural terms—as for instance, apostolic bishops. With the other, diocesan forms of episcopacy and localized modes of ministry, went negative associations—as for instance:

> I wish to warn you against the growing evil of locality in bishops, elders, preachers, or Conferences. Locality is essential to cities and towns, but traveling is as essential to the country.

On which priority Asbury rested was clear. In the same text from which the preceding came, namely his "Valedictory to Bishop William McKendree of 1813," Asbury labored to show that Methodism afforded the only modern instance of apostolic bishops.

By apostolicity he did not intend the unbroken succession of episcopal ordinations claimed by Rome and Anglicans. Rather, he intended the recovery of the religious or spiritual traveling office in Methodism. That made bishops apostolic. He made the case by appealing to the work of the Anglican historian Thomas Haweis. Citing him extensively, Asbury insisted that Methodist bishops fulfilled what Haweis described as the apostolic role—planting and watering:

> We have planted and watered; although our continent is three thousand miles in length, we have measured it year after year, embracing fifty-one or two districts, about six hundred circuits, and nine Annual Conferences, all which, with very few exceptions, we have visited.

We are therefore, Asbury insisted, "apostolic bishops; for we have both planted and watered, and do water still."[13]

> This leads me to conclude that there were no local bishops until the second century; that the apostles, in service, were bishops, and that those who were ordained in the second century mistook their calling when they became local and should have followed those bright examples in the apostolic age. . . .
>
> We have a few more thoughts to add. It is my confirmed opinion that the apostles acted both as bishops and traveling superintendents in planting and watering, ruling and ordering the whole connection; and that they did not ordain any local bishops, but that they ordained local deacons and elders. I feel satisfied we should do the same. . . .
>
> My dear Bishop, it is the traveling apostolic order and ministry that is found in our very constitution. No man among us can locate without order, or forfeit his official standing. No preacher is stationary more than two years; no presiding elder more than four years; and the constitution will remove them; and all are moveable at the pleasure of the superintendent whenever he may find it necessary for the good of the cause.[14]

Some of this argumentation, even as intended for McKendree, served apologetical purposes. However, for Asbury, there was something deeply religious about the traveling itself. Certainly Asbury treated it as a divine

Asbury was unmarried, remember.

imperative, for himself and for others. He disdained other evangelical movements, even the closely aligned German bodies, which did not insist on traveling in the same way. He despaired of those gifted preachers who located. He elevated itinerancy over that sacred bond of marriage. Marriage produced locations. *Must bishops then be celibate?*

Itineration for Asbury possessed elements of that biblical wandering, namely movement itself guided and mandated by God. Traveling, movement, riding, being on the road had an almost mystical quality for Asbury. And the miles logged registered something about the spiritual estate:

[July 1802 New York]

At Rhinebeck I made up four thousand miles, and have one hundred in advance towards the fifth thousand I shall have made since the last of July 1801. Of the little time we have, may be judged by the length of our rides, day after day; yet, at this speed must I go to meet the conferences, and visit the principal societies. My soul is at times greatly drawn out in prayer.[15]

And so, year after year, Asbury measured his wanderings. Superintendency episcopacy entailed spiritual journeying. *what can that mean now?*

Circuits: Corporate Pilgrimage

Asbury's travels, like those of all his preachers, were more than just wanderings. While he wandered to make contact with the Methodist watering places, he also made a circuit to reach each conference, health permitting, and even to attend quarterly meetings when en route. Circuits had something of a pilgrimage quality, a periodicity, a sacred destination to them. For circuits ended in a special corporate gathering, a conference or quarterly conference.

Annual conferences especially took on the character of sacred gatherings and the journeys to them pilgrimage. On the trips out from conferences preachers rode together until the trails to their circuits diverged. On the trips back to conference they fell into together as well, bands of them arriving from the corners of their work. Moving from conference to conference and quarterly meeting to quarterly meeting, Asbury joined and was joined by these entourages of preachers. As he and his companion went along and gathered in those bound for the next conference, they made pilgrimage together. Similar but smaller entourages assembled en route to quarterly conferences. At other times, itinerants rode by themselves and at times Asbury rode with only a small company. Yet even on the remote parts of circuits or on distance rides—when Asbury like the lowly circuit riders made their way alone—they knew they had a yoke-fellow elsewhere on the circuit. And they knew themselves bound for a common destination—conference.

Conference gatherings! These—as we have tried to show—were indeed remarkably renewing, spiritually rich, revivalistic, communal occasions.[16] Something of that Jesse Lee captured in recounting his first conference that of 1782 meeting at Ellis's Meeting House, Sussex:

> The union and brotherly love which I saw among the preachers, exceeded every thing I had ever seen before, and caused me to wish that I was worthy to have a place amongst them. When they took leave of each other, I observed that they embraced each other in their arms, and wept as though they never expected to meet again. Had the heathen been there, they might have well said, "See how these Christians love one another!" By reason of what I saw and heard during the four days that the Conference sat, I found my heart truly humbled in the dust, and my desire greatly increased to love and serve God more publicly than I had ever done before. [17]

Quarterly meetings had even more decidedly a spiritual character, and even general conferences could possess something of that revivalistic spirit. And circuits and conferences linked together to form the connection as a whole—itself a spiritual entity in Asbury's eyes.

So he and Coke could wax eloquent about the connection, about circuits and itinerancy under episcopal direction, about appointments—explaining in their annotations on the *Discipline* why they (the bishops) rather than conferences must station the preachers. The spiritual and the instrumental, grace and efficiency, the mundane and the mysterious mixed together in their brief:

> How could an itinerant ministry be preserved through this extensive continent, if the yearly conferences were to station the preachers? They would, of course, be taken up with the sole consideration of the spiritual and temporal interests of that part of the connection, the direction of which was intrusted to them. The necessary consequence of this mode of proceeding would probably, in less than an age, be the division of the body and the independence of each yearly conference.

The conferences would be more and more estranged from each other for want of a mutual exchange of preachers: and that grand spring, the union of the body at large, by which, under divine grace, the work is more and more extended through this vast country, would be gradually weakened, till at last it might be entirely destroyed. The connection would no more be enabled to send missionaries to the western states and territories, in proportion to their rapid population. The grand circulation of ministers would be at an end, and a mortal stab given to the itinerant plan. The surplus of preachers in one conference could not be drawn out to supply the deficiencies of others, through declensions, locations, deaths, &c. and the revivals in one part of the continent could not be rendered beneficial to the others. Our grand plan, in all its parts, leads to an itinerant ministry. Our bishops are travelling bishops. All the different orders which compose our conferences are employed in the travelling line; and our local preachers are, in some degree, travelling preachers. Everything is kept moving as far as possible; and we will be bold to say, that, next to the grace of God, there is nothing like this for keeping the whole body alive from the centre to the circumference, and for the continual extension of that circumference on every hand.[18]

Traveling, one might argue, constituted Methodism as church. Methodism took its adherents on a corporate pilgrimage. The whole body took this spiritual journey, led by the itinerant general superintendent.

The Quest: Perfection

A third kind of traveling Asbury undertook through his preaching, prayers, spiritual counsel, and exercise of discipline. These constituted the purposes of his physical movement. He traveled in order to preach, complained of dumb days, and gloried in the finding liberty in the spoken word. He moved then to encourage his preachers and people along the spiritual road—from sin and wrath to confession to conversion on to perfection. Indeed, one should say that traveling served really the end of cultivating the Christian life. Asbury traveled for the preaching, the prayers, the spiritual counsel, and the exercise of discipline. His *Journal* says that plainly—over and over and over again—I rode and preached, I rode and preached, I rode and preached. The following entry Asbury replicated thousands of times:

[June 1780]

> I rode to Jenkins's and spoke plainly to about eighty people, and found the word was fitted to their cases; met class; it was a day of peace to me; the Lord was with me at this poor, but good man's house. I was kept by the power of God; my soul is breathing after the Lord at all times.[19]

Traveling carried Asbury, as it carried the Methodist people, ever closer to God. A threefold movement marked the progress. First, there was the movement of the leaders—traveling, perhaps to a class. Second, there was movement by the Methodist people, traveling to quarterly meeting, perhaps a great distance, to stay the two days. Third, there was movement of the Spirit, traveling the Christian life, the *via salutis*, marked out by Mr. Wesley.

We have tended to isolate the latter, the way of salvation, the *via salutis*—to theologize it, to reify it, to interiorize it, to spiritualize it, to treat it in distinction from the traveling that made it possible. But one has only to read the accounts of early Methodism to know that the spiritual and the physical, the emotional and the rational, the interior movement and the exterior, the salvific and the ethical went hand in hand. Something of that is captured in an entry for November 1788:

> At Annamessex quarterly meeting I was at liberty on Rev. iii, 20. Again I preached on, "Fear not, little flock," . . . most of our members in these parts have freed their slaves. [20]

As this entry suggests, Asbury and early Methodism made antislavery one indicator of spiritual attaintment. Antislavery measured progress—as did other Methodist rules—measured progress on the road to perfection.

Traveling with Asbury, then, had its cost, expectations, high standards. Methodists traveled with Asbury through classes, love feasts, quarterly meetings—where discipline, accountability, and devotion aided one on the way to holiness, to perfection, to salvation. So Asbury and Coke could affirm traveling as "that plan, which God has so wonderfully owned, and which is so perfectly consistent with the apostolic and primitive practice."[21] They knew it to be of God. They had cited two pages of the Scripture evidencing the traveling plan.[22] Traveling took Asbury, traveling took Methodists, en route to the promised land.

Itinerancy: Traveling Onward, Toward, Inward

Asbury and early Methodism combined elements of all three kinds of spiritual journeying and invited Americans of various races, languages, classes, ages and both genders to journey to God in distinctively Methodist fashion. And Asbury's successful combining of all three, then, made him a spiritual tutor for the movement. On the most elemental level, then, Asbury's journeying represented fundamental Methodist affirmations about the religious life.

The three kinds of traveling also captured central Methodism affirmations. There are, for instance, rough approximations of free will and human accountability with wandering, free grace with quest, and holiness with pilgrimage. These basic Methodist tenets, these deeper movements of the human spirit, found expression in styles of Methodist physical motion, in Asbury's and early Methodism's traveling. And that traveling had aspects of wandering, quest, and pilgrimage.

Further, the three dimensions of travel evoke fundamental dimensions of Methodist polity and practice. Itineration as wandering—in its circumambulation of the movement as a whole—encompassed Methodism's connnectionalism, as did the office of this special wanderer (the scriptural *episkopos*). The scheduled movement from conference to conference, to quarterly meetings, to class meetings had a pilgrimage character. Its quest dimension took form in the movement toward which Asbury beckoned those who gathered—into a disciplined life, toward holiness, for freedom, even against slavery. And together these three dimensions point to the missional, the evangelistic, and the revivalistic nature of the ministry exercised through itinerancy.

It follows that the traveling also—and we cannot develop this point here, though it has oft been claimed by Methodists—proved remarkably apt for an American society that in its formative decades exploded west from the eastern seaboard. Our national connectionalism, the appointive and circuit system that networked what was nationally encompassed, the evangelistic imperative with which we deployed ourselves, and our discipline that ordered the individuals brought into our connection worked to bring unity and coherence to our people and, one might add, to American society. Methodism grew with the nation rapidly to be the great Protestant American church. Methodists early recognized the fit, that their itinerating ministry had been providentially supplied for the American environment.[23]

In claiming that "fit," Methodists stressed its practicality and effectiveness. They said less about itinerancy's appropriateness to the deeper recesses of our own religious genius. Both deserve remark. Journeying was doubly providential—doubly predestined the Calvinists would say. It did indeed work, fit the American scene, and in no small measure explains our explosive growth. It also fit the fundamental affirmations Methodists made theologically, though neither Asbury nor Wesley fully explored that second fit.

Nor have their followers. We continue to think of traveling, itinerancy—as a tactic—albeit an effective one. But efficiency does not, I think, explain why Methodists made itinerancy one of their central affirmations. In itinerancy, Methodists acted out, dramatized, and displayed their theological values. Itinerancy symbolized Methodism. It had sacramental force.

Asbury's "General" View

That Francis Asbury sustained Wesley's appointive and traveling pattern—the superintending and itinerant aspects of Wesley's *episkopē*—we assume to be well known. Our task with those aspects of episcopacy is to probe for their deeper religious and theological dimensions. Those are, perhaps, the most familiar aspect of Asbury's work and most clearly evocative of Wesley's leadership style. Less obvious, we would guess, are the ways in which Asbury tracked Wesley's "general" office, in particular, his exercise of a teaching role in a connectional fashion.

The Wesleys, John and Charles, taught the people called Methodist. In open fields and small rooms, in addresses for rustic auditors and discourses aimed at the university trained, in texts suited to the meanest intelligence and in selections from the best of the tradition, in items for private study and in hymns for public praise, the Wesleys taught in pervasive, extensive, and systematic fashion.

John Wesley was the teacher for Methodism, Charles its muse. John's especial genius was in creating a literature and media for instruction. His correspondence, tracts, republications of Christian classics, sermons (both delivered and published), controversial and apologetical pieces, magazine, schools, classes and societies, rules, republished libraries, encouragement to families and societies to create libraries, Sunday schools, conference sessions, training and supervision of his assistants and helpers—indeed the entire structure of Methodism—betray a remarkable drive to educate his people in the faith, to identify the heart of the Christian gospel, and to teach the faith. From John, Methodists learned how to say what they believed. From Charles, how to sing it. Both Wesleys consistently taught.

Virtually the entire Wesleyan system functioned educationally and permitted the Wesleys teaching roles. The Wesleys created popular literature for British peoples but also social systems—classes, bands, societies—within which education in the faith could take place, all to the purpose of reforming the church and the nation. In similar fashion, Wesley taught his preachers, most of them not university educated. Through his conferences of preachers he established expectations for self-education, encouraged them in reading, set standards of everyday improvement, and provided guidelines for belief and practice. The latter, *The Large Minutes,* became the *Discipline* of early American Methodism. It functioned for the preachers especially, as for the people more generally, as the syllabus for their education in ministry. It was really a manual for ministry, individual and collective. So, too, the standards that Wesley provided for the American movement functioned as a curriculum—formally established deposits of his teaching and of that of the church traditionally. So his *Explanatory Notes on the New Testament, Standard Sermons,* and modified version of the Anglican *Articles of Religion,* in addition to the *Discipline,* became the touchstones of American Methodist belief and practice.[24]

So Wesley exercised what theologians call the teaching office. Fittingly, he understood himself to be a scriptural *episkopos,* a scriptural bishop for his people. He made Methodism into a giant classroom. And, the activities and structures and processes by which he taught were also what connected Methodists to him and to one another. The educational was connectional. The connectional was educational. At the heart of both was Wesley. This orientation toward the common good kept separatist tendencies in check and allowed the movement to remain within the Church of England during Wesley's lifetime.

Cokesbury

The first two American bishops, Thomas Coke and Francis Asbury, and especially Asbury endeavored with much more modest human and material resources and under frontier conditions, to make comparable provision for American Methodists, to deliver resources and instruction on a nonsectarian basis and to connect the movement through education. They followed Wesley's example, even to the point of starting and restarting Cokesbury College, a school modeled after Wesley's Kingswood.[25]

Coke, attorney and cleric, Oxford educated (B.A., M.A., D.C.L.), sought to exercise Wesley's role fully. He gave American Methodism a measure of intellectual leadership, particularly through his guidance on the crafting of documents, through speaking eloquently on the conference floor, by preaching throughout the connection, and in championing antislavery—so providing ideas for the new American church. These several roles he played most successfully in the period leading up to and immediately following the Christmas Conference. What his stature might have been had he committed himself fully to the American church we can only guess. Thereafter, however, his intellectual leadership dissipated, the consequence of his movement back and forth across the Atlantic, of Asbury's savvy in keeping tight hold on the appointment reins, and of American disenchantment with his tactics, style, and commitments.[26]

Asbury: Teacher?

Asbury, who unlike Coke, remained in America rather than dividing his time between Britain and the United States, more successfully undertook Wesley's popular educational roles.[27]

This would not be our image of the man. We picture him as modestly educated, not a writer, even struggling with his journal. This portrayal remains accurate. Yet, despite meager formal training, he sought to exercise the teaching office, even in literary fashion. He guided the publishing efforts of the movement, issuing directives and counsel to the books agents, first John Dickins and then Ezekiel Cooper. Under his encouragement, the publishers made two efforts at a magazine, the *Arminian Magazine* in 1789 and 1790 and *The Methodist Magazine* in 1797 and 1798. They produced an American version of Wesley's works.[28] They republished British items and a few American originals.[29] They made available annually the *Discipline*, an American version of the *Hymn Book*,[30] *Minutes* of the annual conferences, and eventually a compilation thereof.[31] They also produced or disseminated a stream of Methodist devotional biographies, often knocking off the Wesleyan originals.

Asbury also wrote and published, motivated in part by a teaching impulse. The most important of such efforts was his *Journal*. The earliest parts appeared in serial form in the short-lived American *Arminian Magazine* in 1789 and 1790. They were published in separate form again in 1802.[32] Then again in 1810, he gave attention to the preparation of yet another edition.[33] Something of what he expected from this publication can be inferred from his frequent entries while editing, for instance in 1798:

> I have well considered my journal: it is inelegant; yet it conveys much information of the state of religion and country. It is well suited to common readers; the wise need it not. I have a desire that my journals should be published, at least after my death, if not before. [34]

He thought about the special needs of the American Methodists in his concern for an American hymnody. So he put out his own version of a *Hymn Book*.[35] Asbury resorted to print also to deal with the threats to the unity of the movement. He had worked for some time on a volume that would heal Methodism's wounds. It eventually appeared in time to address the James O'Kelly schism. He entitled it graphically, *The Causes, Evils, and Cures of Heart and Church Divisions, Extracted from the Works of Mr. Jeremiah Burroughs and Mr. Richard Baxter*.[36]

Perhaps the most self-evident exercise of the teaching office came in 1798. In that year as we have already noted, Asbury (with Coke) issued an annotated version of the *Discipline*,[37] an endeavor to instruct the Methodist faithful through and about Methodist belief and practice. They did so in the wake of the fight with James O'Kelly and in response to his sustained criticism of episcopacy. Our several citations from this work, both in the present chapter and in the second, evidence Asbury's success in teaching about the Methodist way and about its modes of leadership.

Asbury endeavored at various other points and through several media to provide Methodism with a self-portrait, a way of understanding itself. He called these efforts history. He conceived both the *Minutes* and the *Discipline* as serving such purposes. Another that he initiated, began with his directives to the presiding elders to give him reports of their districts and the religious state and events therein.

> Once in a year all the presiding elders ought to write to the Episcopacy, to collect into a focus the work of God, for the press, and I wish the

preachers of [today] would write a brief of their conviction, conversion and call to preach and where they had laboured. I will select all the most spiritual parts of letters to print and to keep a history of what God is doing in the South. . . . Would the presiding elders write to me one letter only of the state of the work, I should rejoice and the city preachers also of the cities. We could give great personal information to the conference and individuals of the work of God.[38]

The resulting volume, now quite rare, Asbury entitled, *Extracts of Letters Containing Some Account of the Work of God Since the Year 1800.*[39]

The book agents and Asbury also mimicked Wesley's endeavor to make the system function as school. By making the itinerating preachers agents for the publishing enterprise, they turned all of the circuit system into a giant distribution network.

Asbury played his most important educational roles orally. The aspect of this that is most accessible is his effort to direct the movement through several valedictory statements.[40] More important but elusive than that were his daily interventions—throughout his ministry—in the lives of all those with whom he traveled, resided, spoke. The educational roles in which he probably most succeeded are lost to us—namely through his sermons and prayers, his statements in conference, his conversations, and especially his talks with horseback companions. Asbury taught, as early Methodism taught, in a seminar of the road. He exercised the teaching office preeminently in oral fashion. Unfortunately, the dimensions of this can only be inferred from notations of texts[41] in his *Journal*, from the concerns that prompt his *Letters*, from the chance comment that his companions minute at the end of the day. Thereby he gave intellectual leadership to the Methodist movement.[42]

We do have, however, Asbury's valedictory statements. In these, he waxes eloquent on the apostolic and Wesleyan pattern of general itinerant superintendency. For instance in a long written exhortation in 1816, submitted not long before his death, Asbury turned his attention to the election of additional bishops and the requisites of the office.[43] He insisted on calling "men" to the office who by life experience in the ministry will be equipped to speak effectively to the whole Church:

They must be formed in all things after the pattern shewd us in the mount, able Ministers of the New Testament, real Apostolic men filled with the Holy Ghost. But what our order of things require of them? Not such as can be performed by superannuated or supernumerary preachers, but by men just past the meridian, that have already proved themselves not only servants but mere slaves, *who* with willing minds have taken with cheerfulness and resignation frontier stations, with hard fare, labouring and suffering night and day, hazarding their lives by waters, by lodging indoors and out, and where Indian depredations and murders have been committed once a month or perhaps once a quarter, by *the sides of* the path they have trod, and *in* the houses and cabins *where* they have lodged, and upon some of the persons they have been in social habits and intimacy with, and even *upon* their own brethren of the local and travelling ministry. They ought to be men who can ride at least three thousand miles and meet ten or eleven Conferences in a year, and by their having had a charge of local Conferences from sixty to an hundred Official characters, to have presided in and *to have directed well* all the business of the whole with every member, having received and graduated exhorters, preachers, deacons, and elders in the local line, ready to all the duties of their call-ing, always pleasant, affable, and communicative,—to know how to behave in all company, rich or poor, impious or pious, ministers and professors of our own and all denominations, but more abundantly to remember to the poor the gospel must be preached, and always to con-descend to men of low estate.

This was quite different counsel than that which Coke had offered him. It was counsel drawn out of Asbury's living under the Wesleyan mantle.

Ezekiel Cooper in the biography drawn out of the funeral sermon, well summed up Asbury's exercise of the teaching, the general office:

We have been accustomed to receive the annual visits, of our Asbury, to be benefitted by his public ministry, to be instructed by his lectures and counsels, in society meetings, and to be profited by his pious conversations, and holy examples, in private families, and social circles. . . .

The Bible, to him, was the book of books, and his grand confession of faith. He was careful to regulate, all his religious tenets and doctrines, by the book of God; and to discard every thing that was incompatible with the divine law and testimony. Mr. Wesley's Sermons, and Notes on the Scriptures, and Fletcher's Checks, exemplify his leading doctrines. The Articles of religion, in the Form of Discipline, and, what is com-monly called, the Apostles' Creed, contain a brief summary of his faith and doctrines.—In his public ministry, in his conference communi-cations, and examinations of candidates, for the ministry; in his addresses to the Societies, in his private and social interviews, and in his sentimental conversations; we have often heard him, instructively and entertainingly, profess, declare, and enforce his opinions and doctrines. . . .

He rightly divided the word of truth, and gave to each his portion in due season. He had a doctrine, for the unrighteous impenitent sinner; a doctrine, for the broken hearted penitent mourner; a doctrine, for the believing, humble, loving christian; and, a doctrine, for every situation and station in life; and, for the variety of casuistical cases of conscience, and questions of moral and religious duty, so frequently occurring in the economy and concerns of the Christian life and conduct, in doing and suffering the will of God. He was, in scriptural and casuistical theology, a Master in Israel; and a distinguished evangelical divine. Deservedly to be placed in the first class of patriarchal and apostolical theologians, pastors, and bishops. . . .

Have we not the prototype, or the archetype, of the manner of life, of our late venerable bishop Asbury? That is, the original exemplar, in Paul, of the surprising copy, in Asbury?[44]

Superintendency

Like Asbury's "itinerancy," his "superintendency" has hardly been overlooked. Nor has its import and character been missed. His penchant for obedience, discipline, connection, appointment and all the other various dimensions of order, oversight and superintendence surfaced with his first appearance on the colonial scene and continued till his death. His superintendence the preachers knew well. Indeed, as we have noted, it figured prominently in the significant schisms of early Methodism. On his exercise of authority, Cooper commented extensively:

His episcopal charges, official directions, and constitutional appointments and orders, in general, were punctually observed, and respectfully, willingly, and cheerfully obeyed. Very few, either primitive or modern, ever knew, or acquired the art, better than he, of obtaining, exercising and supporting the pastoral and episcopal influence and authority; and of using it, with so much dignity, respectability, usefulness, and approbation. He had a particular qualification for governing; his peculiar temperature of mind and spirit, his dignified manner of conversation and deportment, his stern reserve, tempered by a social freedom, his authoritative decisions, softened down by gentle soothings, and his apparent inflexibility and independent opinion, placidly yielding to reasonable and amicable accommodations; carried with them an impressive, and almost irresistible influence; and gave him a kind of patriarchal ascendancy and superiority. . . . [45]

Asbury exercised authority adroitly. He also championed Methodism's connectional order. We have already cited several statements in which he insisted on episcopal prerogative because of his conviction that the superintendents alone gained oversight of the whole connection.

He was very clear about the functionality of the Methodist order and of the essential role therein of the superintendents. He also saw this general, connectional superintendency as divinely ordained, as scriptural, as apostolic. For instance, he instructs Bishop William McKendree in 1813:[46]

[To William McKendree] Speaking to the Genesee [New York] Annual Conference in your presence on the subject of apostolical, missionary Methodist Episcopal Church government, I was desired to commit my thoughts to writing. I feel the more disposed to do this, that I may leave a written testimony which may be seen, read, and known when your friend and father is taken from the evil to come. . . .

I am bold to say that the apostolic order of things was lost in the first century, when Church governments were adulterated and had much corruption attached to them. At the Reformation the Reformers only beat off part of the rubbish, which put a stop to the rapid increase of absurdities at that time; but how have they increased since! Recollect that state of the different Churches as it respects government and discipline in the seventeenth century [i.e., eighteenth century] when the Lord raised up that great and good man John Wesley, who formed an evangelical society in England. In 1784 an apostolical form of Church government was formed in the United States of America at the first General Conference of the Methodist Episcopal Church held at Baltimore, in the State of Maryland. . . .

But we must restore and retain primitive order; we must, we will, we have the same doctrine, the same spirituality, the same power in ordinances [sacraments], in ordination, and in spirit. . . .

You will say if our Church were as pure as the primitive Church, will it not, may it not, like other modern [Churches] decline? I answer, we live in a purer age and in a free country. If discipline be maintained, men that carry sand rather than salt for the sheep will be constrained soon to leave us, to join some more honorable, but perhaps fallen, Church, where they can have more ease and greater emoluments. We have lived to see the end of such persons who left us and set up for themselves—witness Hammett and O'Kelly.

And his last word to the church—"Address, Counsel and Advice to the General Conference of the Methodist Episcopal Church, 1816,"[47]—sounded the same theme:

[Near Charleston, S.C.] January 8, 1816

[To the Members of the General Conference]

Most dearly beloved in the Lord:
  My loving confidential Sons in the Gospel of the grace of God, in Christ Jesus, great grace rest upon you. The God of glory cover your assembly and direct all your acts and deliberations for the Apostolic order and establishment of the Church of God in holy succession to the end of time. Only recollect as far as your observation or information will go, what God hath done by us . . . in about 70 years in Europe, and less than 50 years in America, and what wonderful things he may do for us and our successors in future years if we stand fast in the Gospel doctrine and pure Apostolic ordination, discipline and government into which we have been called and now stand.
    We are prepared, and, if called upon, to prove and demonstrate even in your assembly, not from uncertain Church Histories and testimonies, but from the pure Oracles of the New Testament,—Three distinct ordinations, their distinct powers rising in gospel order by constituted degrees, one over another, and under the government, and distinct in names, that is to say Apostles, Elders, and Deacons. We will enter the sanctuary of divine truth, here we shall stand, this is our ground. . . .

Episcopacy As Exemplified in Later Episcopacy

After Asbury died in 1816, itinerant general superintendency underwent gradual changes, despite the constitutional protections so deliberately enacted in 1808. The significant change came without malice or forethought on the part of the bishops or the preachers or the people. It occurred because Asbury lived no longer, because Wesley lived no longer.
   Truth be told, Wesley in Britain and Asbury in America functioned as *the* itinerant general superintendent. Asbury accorded Thomas Coke rhetorical and ceremonial roles—letting Coke write letters of counsel and direction, have his name first on *Minutes* and *Discipline*, preach and preside in conference. When the two superintendents traveled together

Coke might claim the pulpit. However, Asbury ran the show. Coke performed, Asbury governed.[48] Coke did not help his authority in America by his chronic absence. He returned to Britain after the three 1785 American conferences. He came back to the United States in 1787, 1789, and 1791. On his second trip, he arrived with various directives from Wesley, orders that did not sit well with the Americans. The conference responded by redefining the authority of both Coke and Wesley. The Annual Minutes for that year, to the first question, "Who are the superintendents?" stipulated the answer "Thomas Coke, (when present in the States), and Francis Asbury." Coke responded by promising not to exercise superintending authority when absent and limiting it when present to ordaining, presiding, and traveling. This conference also rescinded the binding minute of loyalty to Wesley from the *Discipline*, sometimes described as dropping Wesley's name from the Minutes.[49]

The conference's declaration and Coke's concession set precedent and pattern for Asbury's relation to colleagues. The other bishops elected to serve with Asbury enjoyed the same secondary status as Coke, albeit without the formal or legislated restriction. Richard Whatcoat and William McKendree functioned effectively but in Asbury's shadow. At Asbury's death, some of the primacy that Wesley and Asbury had enjoyed did remain with William McKendree, so argues James Kirby. McKendree, the first American-born elected to the office, had taken important initiatives while Asbury lived, the most notable being the episcopal address to general conference, an innovation that took Asbury by surprise. James Kirby calls McKendree "the last itinerant general superintendent."

A House Divided

After the election of Enoch George and Robert R. Roberts in 1816, the three bishops agreed to divide the itineration among themselves instead of moving together through the conferences. This decision constituted the first big first step, Kirby suggests, toward a modified version of diocesan episcopacy. Kirby takes particular note of the politicization and regionalization so powerfully operative in the episcopal elections of 1824 (Joshua Soule and Elijah Hedding). And he views a surrender of the principle of itinerant general superintendency as dramatically played out in the five bishops' unwillingness or inability over the next quadrennia to arrange conference assignments so as to deploy themselves individually and collectively over the whole connection. He also recognizes in that embrace of regionalism—that effective stationing of themselves region-ally—*the* division of the Church, preparatory for 1844.

At whatever point we identify our episcopacy as having given up the Wesleyan form—and whether it has even today—we can certainly take seriously the assumption with which Kirby operates and that has informed this review.

The clear implication is that the more full-fledged the itinerancy, the more extensive the travel, the more thorough the movement across the whole connec-tion—the more general the superintendency, the larger the perspective, the hori-zon, the perception, the understanding of our leadership.

The issue raised by Kirby one might see as before The United Methodist Church once again in the proposal for a four-year presidency of the Council of Bishops. That proposal would seemingly restore what the Church had in Wesley, in Asbury, and to a lesser extent, in McKendree—one person whose figure, voice, and movement dramatized itinerant general superintendency. But what implications follow for other bishops, those not elected to the presidency of the Council?

The question before the bishops and Church resembles to some degree the issues faced after the death of Asbury and with the election of a group of bishops who enjoyed parity among themselves. Could five bishops, no one of them an Asbury over the others—could the bishops as peers—pro-vide the *episkopē*, the general *episkopē*, that the constitution called for? And could it be provided without riding over the whole? If not, how was that general *episkopē* to be received by the conference(s) over which individual bishops presided? It could not be, so Kirby argues, and division resulted.

The question for today is a variant or perhaps the inverse of that for the 1820s. If there be one bishop, in effect riding or presiding over the whole, do the others retain their general office? And how do their con-ferences receive the general *episkopē* promised in the office, the itinerant general superintendency?

It is, of course, possible to conclude with Kirby that Methodism adopted the diocesan principle after Asbury and has been living ever more into its reality.

We would like to hold out the hope that the principle of itinerant gen-eral superintendency can take and, to some degree, has taken new expres-sion in what the bishops have been able to do collectively through the

Council. We concur in worrying with Kirby over the fateful consequences of the abandonment of general itinerancy on the part of all the bishops and of believing that our Church would gain much were they to be stationed nationally rather than jurisdictionally.[50]

We share with him the conviction that the more general the itinerancy—the more general the superintendency, the larger the perspective, the horizon, the perception, the understanding of our leadership—the more fully Wesleyan the form of *episkopē*.

Fascinating if a bit Romantic. [handwritten annotation]

Notes

1. Robert E. Cushman entitled his essay on this topic, *John Wesley's Experimental Divinity* (Nashville: Kingswood/Abingdon Press, 1989); see also Thomas A. Langford's *Practical Divinity: Theology in the Wesleyan Tradition* (Nashville: Abingdon Press, 1983). Albert C. Outler termed Wesley's "a folk theology" in *John Wesley* (New York: Oxford University Press, 1964), p. vii.

2. *A Collection of Hymns for the Use of the People Called Methodists*, 1780, Preface. See in *Works*, 7: 3, 55-61, 74, 77-78. See also Karen B. Westerfield Tucker, *American Methodist Worship* (New York: Oxford University Press, 2001), pp. 156-75.

3. *The Journal and Letters of Francis Asbury*, 3 vols. ed. Elmer T. Clark et al. (London: Epworth Press; Nashville: Abingdon Press, 1958), hereinafter *JLFA*, III, p. 114, letter dated December 1792 "To Jesse Nicholson." The presiding elder was the counterpart to today's district superintendent. The short titles employed here for standard Methodist reference items, such as this one for volume 3 of Asbury's *Journal and Letters*, are those now recognized by Abingdon Press for the Kingswood productions.

4. *The Substance of a Funeral Discourse . . . on the Death of the Rev. Francis Asbury* (Philadelphia: J. Pounder, 1819). We are also reminded constantly by our colleague Kenneth Rowe of Asbury's darker side—of his compromise on slavery, of his insensitivity to the Germans, of his autocratic power, of his controlling bearing. One has only to read the letters of Thomas Coke or Jesse Lee to appreciate that Asbury's strengths were experienced diversely.

5. *The Journal and Letters of Francis Asbury [JLFA]*.

6. *JLFA*, I, p. 10, November 19 and 21, 1771.

7. *JLFA*, I, p. 357 in North Carolina, June 17, 1780.

8. *JLFA*, III, p. 93, in a letter to Bishop Coke, 1791.

9. Thomas Coke and Francis Asbury, *The Doctrines and Disciplines of the Methodist Episcopal Church in America* (Philadelphia: Henry Tuckniss, 1798), p. 45.

10. *JLFA*, III, p. 465, "To Mrs. Ann Willis," 1812.

11. "A wandering Aramean was my ancestor; he went down into Egypt and lived there as an alien, few in number, and there he became a great nation, mighty and populous. When the Egyptians treated us harshly and afflicted us, by imposing hard labor on us, we cried to the LORD, the God of our ancestors; the LORD heard our voice and saw our affliction, our toil, and our oppression. The LORD brought us out of Egypt with a mighty hand

and an outstretched arm, with a terrifying display of power, and with signs and wonders; and he brought us into this place and gave us this land, a land flowing with milk and honey. So now I bring the first of the fruit of the ground" (Deuteronomy 26:4-10). The typology I owe to Wesley Kort, formerly a colleague in religious studies at Duke University.

12. Coke and Asbury, *The Doctrines and Disciplines of the Methodist Episcopal Church, in America,* p. 36.

13. JLFA, August 5, 1813, "A Valedictory Address to William McKendree," pp. 475-92. Several pages into the address, Asbury began to appeal by extensive citation to Thomas Haweis's *History of the Church of Christ,* on the basis of which he posited the apostolic character of Methodist episcopacy.

14. Francis Asbury, "Valedictory Address to William McKendree," *JLFA,* III, 1813, pp. 475-92; excerpts, especially pp. 487, 492.

15. JLFA, II, p. 353.

16. Richey, *The Methodist Conference in America: A History* (Nashville: Kingswood Books/Abingdon Press, 1996); Frank, *Polity, Practice, and the Mission of The United Methodist Church,* updated edition (Nashville: Abingdon Press, 2002).

17. Minton Thrift, *Memoir of the Rev. Jesse Lee with Extracts from his Journals* (New York: N. Bangs and T. Mason for the Methodist Episcopal Church, 1823), p. 42.

18. Coke and Asbury, *The Doctrines and Disciplines of the Methodist Episcopal Church, in America,* pp. 41-42.

19. JLFA, I, p. 359. He was in North Carolina at the time.

20. JLFA, I, p. 582.

21. Coke and Asbury, *The Doctrines and Disciplines of the Methodist Episcopal Church, in America,* p. 36.

22. Ibid., pp. 35-36.

23. On this point see Nathan O. Hatch, *The Democratization of American Christianity* (New Haven and London: Yale University Press, 1989); and for a more perverse reading, Roger Finke and Rodney Stark, *The Churching of America, 1776–1990* (New Brunswick, N.J.: Rutgers University Press, 1992).

24. Controversy continues over what constitute United Methodist standards. See especially, Richard P. Heitzenrater, "At Full Liberty: Doctrinal Standards in Early American Methodism," *Quarterly Review* 5 (Fall 1985): 6-27; also in *Doctrine and Theology in The United Methodist Church,* ed. Thomas A. Langford (Nashville: Kingswood Books, 1991) pp. 109-42; Thomas C. Oden's response, "What Are 'Established Standards of Doctrine'? A Response to Richard Heitzenrater," *Quarterly Review* 7 (Spring 1987): 42-62. See Oden's further elaboration in *Doctrinal Standards in the Wesleyan Tradition* (Grand Rapids: Francis Asbury Press of Zondervan Publishing House, 1988); and in *The Trust Clause Governing Use of Property in The United Methodist Church,* an online book available at http://goodnewsmag.org/news/122902Trust Clause_FULL.pdf (or htm). Also pertinent are Robert E. Cushman, *John Wesley's Experimental Divinity: Studies in Methodist Doctrinal Standards* (Nashville: Kingswood Books/Abingdon Press, 1989); *Wesley and the Quadrilateral: Renewing the Conversation,* ed. W. Stephen Gunter et al. (Nashville: Abingdon Press, 1998); and *Doctrines and Discipline: Methodist Theology and Practice,* eds. Dennis M. Campbell, William B. Lawrence, and Russell E. Richey (Nashville: Abingdon Press, 1999).

Much more written than makes clear.

25. On this venture and Methodist education generally, see Francis I. Moats, "The Educational Policy of The Methodist Episcopal Church Prior to 1860" (Ph.D. thesis, Graduate College of the State University of Iowa, 1926), pp. 38-56; A. W. Cummings, *The Early Schools of Methodism* (New York: Phillips and Hunt, 1886); Sylvanus M. Duvall, *The Methodist Episcopal Church and Education Up to 1869* (New York: Bureau of Publications, Teachers College, 1928); Robert H. Conn with Michael Nickerson, *A Handbook for Higher Education and Campus Ministry in the Annual Conference*, foreword by F. Thomas Trotter (Nashville: Division of Higher Education, 1989).

26. On Coke's leadership intentions and ambitions, see Warren Thomas Smith, "Thomas Coke's Contribution to the Christmas Conference: A Study in Ecclesiology," *Rethinking Methodist History*, eds. Russell E. Richey and Kenneth E. Rowe (Nashville: Kingswood Books, 1985), pp. 37-47. The definitive treatment is John Vickers, *Thomas Coke: Apostle of Methodism* (Nashville: Abingdon Press, 1969).

27. This discussion distills treatment of Asbury in "The Legacy of Francis Asbury: The Teaching Office in Episcopal Methodism," *Quarterly Review* 15 (Summer 1995): 145-74.

28. *JLFA*, III, p. 323, letter to Ezekiel Cooper, July 26, 1805.

29. See James Penn Pilkington, *The Methodist Publishing House*, I (Nashville: Abingdon Press, 1968), pp. 51-154.

30. *JLFA*, III, pp. 232-33, letter to Ezekiel Cooper, the book agent, dated Dec. 31, 1801. There he spoke about his several publishing ventures. The preface to the hymnal appears in III, pp. 397-98. For Asbury's personal efforts in its creation, see entries in II, p. 554 for Aug. 1807; p. 558 for Oct. 25, 1807; and p. 559 for Nov. 4, 6, 1807.

31. They also produced several Asbury items: his *Journal*, initially serialized, and then as an independent book; a compilation intended to address the James O'Kelly schism, entitled graphically, *The Causes, Evils, and Cures of Heart and Church Divisions, Extracted from the Works of Mr. Jeremiah Burroughs and Mr. Richard Baxter* (Philadelphia, 1792; republished in 1817 and 1849); and Asbury's effort at a history of the movement, *Extracts of Letters Containing Some Account of the Work of God Since the Year 1800* (New York, 1805). The latter's subtitle read *Written By the Preachers and Members of the Methodist Episcopal Church to their Bishops*. Also a joint venture was an annotated version of the *Discipline*, an endeavor to instruct the Methodist faithful through and about Methodist belief and practice. Its full title was *The Doctrines and Discipline of the Methodist Episcopal Church in America with Explanatory Notes By Thomas Coke and Francis Asbury* (Philadelphia, 1798; facsimile edition, ed. Frederick A. Norwood, Rutland, Vt.: Academy Books, 1979).

32. *JLFA*, II for April 5, 1802, pp. 332-33. Asbury complained that he did not get a chance to edit and correct the copy before it was printed.

33. *JLFA*, III, p. 426, letter to Nelson Reed, dated March 22, 1810. Asbury noted that he had spent five or six days reviewing and correcting 1,000 pages of his journal. "Every thing personal, geographical, and prolix will go out, the most spiritual, and historical parts will be reserved." See Elmer T. Clark's "Introduction," I, pp. xv-xviii for discussion of editions of the *Journal*.

34. *JLFA*, II, p. 153, for Feb. 6, 1798.

35. *JLFA*, III, pp. 232-33, letter to Ezekiel Cooper, the book agent, dated Dec. 31, 1801. There he spoke about his several publishing ventures. The preface to the hymnal appears in III, pp. 397-98. For Asbury's personal efforts in its creation, see entries in II, p. 554 for Aug. 1807; p. 558 for Oct. 25, 1807; p. 559 for Nov. 4, 6, 1807.

36. Philadelphia, 1792; republished in 1817 and 1849.

37. *The Doctrines and Discipline of the Methodist Episcopal Church in America with Explanatory Notes, by Thomas Coke and Francis Asbury* (Philadelphia, 1798; facsimile edition, ed. Frederick A. Norwood, Rutland, Vt.: Academy Books, 1979).

38. *JLFA*, III, p. 199, letter to George Roberts, Feb. 4, 1801. Compare letter two days later to Thomas Morrell, III, p. 202:

> You will favour me with a letter to Norfolk, the last of March. If the presiding elders, in the cities and towns and country would give me once a year circumstantial accounts of the work. I would —— —— —— annually of Methodism, like Prince's History for a select collection of original papers.

39. (New York, 1805). The subtitle read *Written By the Preachers and Members of the Methodist Episcopal Church to Their Bishops*.

40. See *JLFA*, II, pp. 739-40 for Aug. 1, 1813; III, pp. 475-92 for Aug. 5, 1813; II, p. 744 for Oct. 29, 1813; *Methodist History*, I, pp. 56-58 for Sept. 29, 1815; and JLFA, III for Jan. 8, 1816.

41. See *JLFA*, "Index of Sermon Texts," III, pp. 818-24. It is worth remarking that Asbury preached on the whole Bible.

42. The immediately preceding paragraphs are taken from "University and Church: Notes on the Methodist Experience," pp. 2-4.

43. Francis Asbury, "Address, Counsel and Advice to the General Conference of the Methodist Episcopal Church, 1816," *JLFA*, III, pp. 532, 540-41.

44. Ezekiel Cooper, *The Substance of a Funeral Discourse . . . on the Death of the Rev. Francis Asbury* (Philadelphia, 1819). Excerpts pp. 27-28, 40-41, 51-52, 59-60, 71, 112, 118-27, 130, 179, 180-81, 185.

45. Cooper, *The Substance of a Funeral Discourse . . . on the Death of the Rev. Francis Asbury*, pp. 40-41, 51-52.

46. Francis Asbury, "Valedictory Address to William McKendree," *JLFA*, III, 1813, pp. 475-92. Excerpts.

47. Francis Asbury, "Address, Counsel and Advice to the General Conference of the Methodist Episcopal Church, 1816," *JLFA*, III, pp. 532, 540-41.

48. *JLFA*, I, pp. 535-39. Note Asbury's account of his sermons on Isaiah 64:1-5 and Romans 10:14-15 in *MEA*, 1789a.

49. See the letter of April 1787 from O'Kelly in *JFLA*, III, pp. 49-54; *Minutes of the Methodist Conferences* (1813), 1786, p. 61; 1787: pp. 62-68; *Sketches of The Life and Travels of Rev. Thomas Ware*, pp. 129-31; Lee, *Short History*, p. 125, MEA, 1785a, Q.2.

50. Kirby, *The Episcopacy in American Methodism*, pp. 85, 97-99, 101-7.

Frank

CHAPTER FOUR

Polity and Practice of Episcopacy in the Contemporary United Methodist Church

I n order to address the question of how to enhance the office and leadership of bishops in the Church, we have to examine contemporary polity and practice. Too many proposals for reform do not take account of basic constitutional principles, or the generations of practice, reform, and wisdom already present in our denominational Church law. At the same time, a look at contemporary polity may open fresh perspectives on unrealized opportunities for making the most of the episcopal office in the Church.

The Character of Methodism

Episcopacy in the United Methodist tradition has been the subject of astonishingly little theological and ecclesiological discussion. Few books have been published on the episcopacy since the vigorous apologetics for Methodism in the nineteenth century. Most twentieth-century literature has been descriptive or narrative in focus. Biographies and autobiographies of bishops for the most part record the stories and anecdotes of a lifetime's interaction with people. Rarely do they venture into the terrain of foundations or rationales for the episcopal office in the Church. The reader of this literature almost gets the sense that it would be considered impolite or impolitic to examine episcopacy more critically or to try to state its ecclesiological purpose.

American Methodism is, after all, a popular tradition. It began as a kind of English church for the common people, deliberately disassociating its clergy from educated elites and its bishops from the landed gentry. It adopted the sacramental rituals of the *Book of Common Prayer* and the traditional Anglican offices of bishop, presbyter, and deacon, but it adapted these forms to the needs of a popular movement. Methodism did not *have* a mission—it *was* a mission movement of starting new class meetings and worshiping congregations wherever the people went across the developing American landscape.

The episcopal office in such a movement was bound to be more informal and flexible than its Anglican predecessor. Traditional bishops' garb was not practical for riding horseback thousands of miles each year and preaching outdoors or in simple frame buildings. Congregations of merchants, tradesmen, and farmers were not expecting ceremony, nor did conferences of circuit-riding preachers wish to be presided over by status-conscious ritualists. When contemporary bishops tell jokes about their office to tease the deference attached to it, or cut the communion ritual short to allow more time for fellowship, or use a teaching session to tell stories instead of framing critical theological issues for the Church, they are expressing this enduring ethos of Methodist populism.

Methodism did not become a peculiar kind of church solely through its populist character, though. Particularly from the standpoint of its itinerant ministry, it was more a kind of preaching order than a church. Candidates for preaching ministry had first to be elected to membership in a conference before they could be ordained. Their status as ordained clergy was always secondary to their covenant relationship with other preaching ministers who had taken the vow of submission to the appointive power of the bishop. Agreeing to go where sent took priority over any commitment to practices for which one is specifically ordained, particularly celebration of the eucharist.

This order of itinerant preachers had a companion form in the class meetings and later the Sunday school classes of the laity. These were led by laity and organized around disciplines that would encourage people in holy living, helping them grow in the knowledge and love of God through their everyday lives. Given the fascination of John Wesley and other early Methodists with the origins and practices of monastic life, it is hardly a stretch to think of Methodism as a kind of monastic covenant community for ordinary people. The means of grace—daily prayer, Scripture study, Christian conversation—were to be practiced by people living the common life of work, school, neighborhood, home, and family.

The character of Methodism as a kind of secularized monasticism gave its bishop's role some of the features of an abbot or head of an order. The seventh century Rule of St. Benedict puts the abbot in the "place of Christ" for the monk and expects that the monk will obey the abbot "as if the order came from God himself." While Methodist people would not have used such expressions (*viz.*, the populism discussed above), nonetheless they have expected that the bishop would represent the unity of their movement in Christ. They have often searched the actions of a bishop for the will of God and accepted ministerial appointments from the bishop as God's leading (however obscure it might seem at times). Their faith has led them to anticipate that Christ might be veiled in the one who assigns the preachers to their places. Their faith strengthens their determination to discern Christ in the actions of the bishop (as for a monk, the abbot), so much the more so for the bishop who is obviously mistaken, fallible, and imperfect.[1]

These roots of Methodism's peculiar episcopacy—the bishop as missionary in a popular movement, the bishop as head of a quasi-monastic order—offer two ways to account for the strange silence of today's *Discipline* on the ecclesiology and polity of episcopacy. United Methodism stands in a long heritage of simply not writing anything down about the theological foundations of episcopacy. The UMC has done little to develop a fixed ecclesiology for the office of bishop (or for the local church, or any other entity), preferring to let episcopacy continue as a practice with the flexibility to adapt to the changing circumstances of the Church's mission. The episcopacy is constitutional, along with conference one of the two constitutional principles of the UMC.[2] But it is constitutional not for ecclesiological reasons—that episcopacy is of the essence of the Church, that there is no Church without bishops—but because of its grounding in the character of Methodism as a movement led by an itinerant order of preachers and forming a laity covenanted for growth in holiness.

Elements associated with the role of bishops for many centuries of Christendom have little part in United Methodist episcopacy. The original presidency of the bishop was at the eucharistic table, where he (for many centuries always he) stood in the place of Christ as a symbolic presence celebrating the Lord's Supper. The bishop's ordinations of presbyter-priests extended to them this sacramental authority. All of the bishop's actions on behalf of the unity and witness of the Church had their foundation in presiding at the one table of the Lord.

Methodists did not see their bishops as primary sacramental figures. Bishops were of the same order as other elders (presbyters) and had no further Sacramental role constitutive of their position. Even today the episcopal powers laid out in the UM constitution have nothing to say about the Sacraments or ordination to administer them.[3]

Yet United Methodism does constitute an episcopal role of presidency, unity, and presence. The bishop presides—at the table, like other elders, to be sure—but primarily in conference. When United Methodists gather to seek the means of grace in Christian conversation and conference, the figure to whom they turn to make this possible is their presiding officer, the bishop. All the diverse voices of the churches, often contentious and passionate in their convictions, look to the bishop for order, fair process, and a framework and spirit of interaction that will make Christian community possible.

For all United Methodists, but especially for the "traveling preachers," the bishop is an emblem of unity in the movement and the order. Elected from among the order of preachers, the bishop emerges as *primus inter pares* (first among equals) in the community of those who share in the covenant of itinerancy. The bishop's making and fixing of appointments expresses the common life of the order. This hardly means that everyone leaves conference with warm feelings or that everyone is united in recognizing the bishop's appointive genius. Just as the bishop traditionally symbolizes the unity of the Church even when it is deeply broken and divided, so the UM bishop is an emblem of the movement's unity even when there is no unanimity.

What seals these roles of presidency and unity is the bishop's presence. While not sacramental in itself, it is still a presence charged with a significance that bears the spirit of the movement. The bishop's role is fulfilled as she or he is simply physically present in as many places and times as possible. As we have argued in chapter 2, the travel required for this level of omnipresence was for the early bishops a sacramental act. Their itinerancy itself was their witness to the power of God and the saving grace of Christ. Their travel made their physical presence possible, as it made the whole movement metaphorically present to itself through the symbol of their office. And in presence is an affirmation of the unity of the Church in Christ, even if only—as in the bread and cup—in the broken, visible forms at hand.

Since 1808 the constitution has established and protected "the plan of our itinerant general superintendency." The word "plan" resonates with the characteristically Methodist understanding of presidency, unity, and . presence. Not so much the office of bishop per se, but the plan of superintendency is protected. The plan is a design in motion, the practice of an episcopacy for a movement—not for an established, organic tradition of church but for a movement within the Church. The conduct of this episcopal plan for a movement requires constant travel and presence in many places, assignment of hundreds of traveling preachers under the bishop's care, and presidency over the occasional assemblies of Methodist people in conference.

Functions of Episcopacy and the UM Office of Bishop

Just as Methodist episcopacy has not been grounded essentially in eucharistic presidency, so more broadly it has not embraced many of the powers traditionally associated with bishops. In contemporary United Methodism, the powers of *episkopē*—the oversight or supervisory function in the Church—are only partially identified with *episkopoi*—the actual office and person of bishops.[4] Even though oversight defines the office of bishop, in actuality many other church bodies are authorized for *episkopē* and the bishop works in tandem with these bodies in order to fulfill the function.

The UM constitution grants to the Council of Bishops "general oversight and promotion of the temporal and spiritual interests of the entire Church." However, the very next phrase demonstrates that this general oversight is shared with the General Conference—"and for carrying into effect the rules, regulations, and responsibilities prescribed and enjoined by the General Conference" (¶ 45). Since General Conference has "full legislative power over all matters distinctively connectional," including the power "to define and fix the powers, duties, and privileges of the episcopacy," clearly the oversight with which bishops are charged is shared with the conference if not derived from it.

The balance of these two constitutional principles—conference and episcopacy—has been a constant point of tension through Methodist history, and understandably so. Increasingly across the generations Methodism has provided clergy and laity assembled in conference the rights and privileges, authority and power to exercise *episkopē* along with bishops. Many of the powers traditionally associated with the office of bishop, largely intact in Roman Catholicism today, are delegated to conference in United Methodism. Only General Conference can speak for the UMC or alter official Church teachings, a function that belongs to the episcopal *magisterium* in Roman Catholic tradition. Only the clergy members of an annual conference can appraise the call and qualifications of candidates for ordained ministry, vote them into conference membership, and authorize their ordination. Unlike the bishops of traditional episcopal churches, UM bishops have no official say in the matter and can refuse to ordain a candidate only if they rule that church law is in some way being transgressed. Bishops are elected, not chosen by other bishops, with laity and clergy participating in the election. Even the assignment of bishops to their episcopal areas is carried out by a conference committee of laity and clergy, the Jurisdictional Committee on Episcopacy, not by the bishops themselves. The power of bishops to "arrange the plan of episcopal supervision of the annual conferences" (¶ 46) is a remnant of episcopal practice predating The Methodist Church and is today limited to rare and exceptional circumstances.

Many powers that once were exercised by Methodist bishops have been delegated to other bodies in the UMC. At one time, bishops practiced the traditional teaching office by selecting and authorizing the curricular course of study for preparing for ordained ministry. This power now belongs to an agency of General Conference. In early Methodism, bishops ruled on matters of church law and judged the constitutionality of General Conference actions. While this power was designated to the General Conference itself by the 1840s in northern Methodism, it continued in the bishops' hands until the 1930s in southern Methodism. Only then was this power of judicial review vested in a new Judicial Council comprised of clergy and laity, with bishops having only the right (but not an exclusive right) to nominate candidates for the Council. The election belongs to General Conference. In the bodies preceding United Methodism's creation in 1968, bishops had broad powers of nomination for members of the general boards and agencies created by General Conference. In the UMC the bishop serves only as a member of an annual conference nominating committee comprised of clergy and laity that forwards names for a jurisdictional pool of nominees (¶ 705). The only annual conference body to which the bishop appoints members is the conference committee on episcopacy, but only one-fifth of them (¶ 634.1). The only body for which the bishop nominates members is the annual conference Board of Ordained Ministry, and even here the nominations are in consultation with the board and the cabinet (¶ 632.1.a). The elections in both cases belong to the annual conference.

Episkopē in United Methodism is also conciliar in nature. The Judicial Council is a constitutional body, not a creation of General Conference, and has final review of all matters of church law. Two other councils of "review and oversight" have been created by General Conference (¶ 703.1). The General Council on Ministries has power "to facilitate the Church's program life as determined by the General Conference," a power belonging to *episkopē* at least as much as the bishops' power "for carrying into effect" what General Conference adopts (¶ 904). The General Council on Finance and Administration develops and reviews budgets for all general church expenditures with accountability and amenability directly to General Conference (¶ 806). All of these councils are comprised of clergy and laity, with bishops serving as members only of GCOM and GCFA.

The Council of Bishops, like the Judicial Council, is a constitutional body and not a creation of General Conference. The *episkopē* it exercises is conciliar, not individual. As Bishop James Mathews stated it,

> *Bishops*, not *a* bishop, are administrative and executive heads of the church. . . . One office of general oversight is shared by a number of persons; collectively they are charged with the temporal and spiritual interests of the whole church.[5]

This statement makes clear that the bishops' oversight is shared, collective, and conciliar, not hierarchical, authoritarian, or individual. As the *Discipline* states it, "The Council of Bishops is thus the collegial expression of episcopal leadership in the Church and through the Church into the world" (¶ 427).

It is difficult to say, however, what the metaphor "heads" means in Mathews's claim, or the term "executive." Neither term is used in the constitution or elsewhere in the *Discipline* to describe the bishops' powers.

The constitution empowers bishops with "carrying into effect" what General Conference "prescribed and enjoined" (¶ 45), while legislative paragraphs charge the bishops with "ordering the life of the Church" (¶ 401). But this is the language of a covenant community of shared discipline, more resonant with the role of an abbot than with oligarchy, military hierarchy, or bureaucratic pyramid.

Ambiguity in defining the bishops' oversight has often led to the use of executive terminology. Many interpreters have called episcopacy the executive branch of government in parallel to the United States presidency. But the office of president bears little resemblance to UM episcopacy. Bishops have no program and propose no legislation. They do not appoint the heads of administrative agencies and have limited powers of nomination. They have few sanctions at their disposal, and certainly no right to fire the people they work with.

Neither, of course, do the bishops have legislative or judicial authority—the other two branches of government. They have no vote in any conference, only in their own council, and even their decisions of church law made in the course of presiding over conference are subject to final review by Judicial Council. So if that doesn't leave executive authority, what does remain as the substance of the bishops' *episkopē?* The constitution offers only the "plan of itinerant general superintendency" to be mined for guidance.

Episkopē as Itinerant

Travel is essential to the practice of episcopacy in United Methodism, and nobody travels quite like the bishops. Their presence in many times and places symbolizes the unity and continuity of the movement. If one thought of every bishop as trailing a strand of yarn wherever she went, one could imagine the bishops' constant travel as a kind of weaving together of the fabric of a widely scattered and diverse community.

The other bodies that share oversight functions are not present in the same way to the whole Church. Conferences are relatively fleeting moments of assembly that carry out their constitutional duties but then disperse. They do not exist when they are not actually meeting, for they have no executive agencies authorized to take any initiative on their behalf. When conferences adjourn, they are no more, and one conference cannot bind the next one. They alone would not be enough to give coherence and consistency to the Church's ministries. Judicial Council is intentionally isolated in order to make the most dispassionate judgments of church law possible (see ¶ 2607 on confidentiality). GCOM and GCFA both have offices and a staff to carry out their mandates, which is more than one can say for the Council of Bishops. Through publications, Web sites, and public meetings they make their work and services known. But in some sense, precisely because the bishops are not administrators of programs, they are present to the Church in a different way—more literally through their constant travel and comprehensive knowledge of the people and places of United Methodism.

The *Discipline* conceives of the bishops' itinerant ministry as collegial and conciliar. In one of the book's more puzzling sentences, it charges the bishops "to travel through the connection at large as the Council of Bishops to implement strategy for the concerns of the Church" (¶ 414.5). Since the Council does not travel as a group, this can only mean that as individual bishops move around the connection they are helping to weave a fabric of connection made up of strands from all the bishops. Each bishop represents the whole conciliar itinerancy as well. In Bishop Mathews's words, "Wherever one bishop is, the whole of episcopacy is there in his or her person."[6] The itinerant office is conciliar, surpassing any single individual and at the same time represented in the person of a particular bishop.

What is present in the bishop as she travels is the connection itself. The bishop represents the common ministry, shared mission, network of institutions, and fabric of relationships that comprises the UM connection. The *Discipline*'s charge "to implement strategy" is oddly aggressive and overreaching in its implication that bishops either have a collective strategy for the Church, or that this kind of executive control is the reason for their travel. They itinerate not to see that "things are getting done," but to be the embodiment of connection in each place—thus encouraging and building up the body for its ministry and mission. They give the movement cohesion, support its morale, and inspire it for connectional action.

Episkopē as General

The constitution grants bishops "general oversight" of the UMC and correlates the office with the actions of General Conference for the connection as a whole. General oversight is conciliar, a matter for the Council of Bishops to "plan" (¶ 45). This *episkopē* for the connection is shared by other councils, as noted above; and as General Conference itself reviews "all matters distinctively connectional" (¶ 15), it also carries out general oversight.

At the same time, no other body has quite the comprehensive overview of United Methodism as a whole as do the bishops in council. A recent Council agenda embraced an enormous range of topics, including review of the Church's work in Africa, Korea, the Middle East, and Puerto Rico, planning for the bishops' initiative on children and poverty, discussion of the relationship of the UMC to other denominations, continuing work toward racial reconciliation, arrangements for bishops to visit UM work in various parts of the world, and adoption of the Council's own structure and budget. The Council continued work on a statement about the purposes of theological education and did more planning for its next episcopal initiative. All this was jammed into a five-day meeting for which some bishops arrived late and some left early because of other travel commitments.

The Council itself is a microcosm of the general Church, with bishops coming from all regions of the United States and many other countries. Warm bonds of fellowship mark their gathering, since bishops have no other peers or membership in the Church outside their own Council. Their gathering also exposes the fractures that divide the UMC as a whole between rich and poor, United States, Europe, Africa, and the Philippines, so-called conservative and so-called liberal points of view, and many other differences. Precisely in the bishops' general view acquired and sustained through their Council is one major hope of reaching across these divisions and finding unity in diversity.

Since the creation of The Methodist Church in 1939, though, many people have questioned what general oversight means for contemporary bishops. This is first of all a geographic issue with consequences for episcopal jurisdiction, in the sense of the scope of episcopal powers and duties under church law. In the church union of 1939, the General Conference delegated to regional and racial jurisdictions its historic power to elect bishops. It also confined the jurisdiction of bishops—their scope of authority for "residential and presidential supervision" under church law—to the regional jurisdiction in which they were elected (¶ 47).

A related but now-forgotten change after 1939 was the disciplinary requirement that a bishop preside and make appointments in the annual conference(s) of his residency for all four years of a quadrennium. This ended a long-standing practice of presiding for three out of four years, with a fellow bishop designated to preside and make the appointments in one year out of the four. The system of episcopal areas that mandated a bishop's residence in a certain city and presidency over conferences contiguous to that residence was now firmly in place.

This regionalization of episcopacy in the U.S. has become even more prominent in recent years. Most bishops now preside over only one annual conference with their episcopal residence in the bounds of that conference. This identifies the bishop even more closely with one region—often coincident with the boundaries of a civil state—and offers even less reason for bishops to visit one another's conferences to preside if only for a day.

Many interpreters have viewed regionalization as a trend toward "diocesan" episcopacy. The 1960–1964 General Conference study of the episcopacy devoted a whole section to the concern of bishops and others that Methodist bishops were becoming "diocesan."[7] In his recent history, James Kirby wondered if the bishop was "a general superintendent with responsibility for a global church or a diocesan executive expected to attend to and promote local issues?"[8] But a United Methodist annual conference bears little resemblance to what other episcopal traditions mean by a diocese. Just as UM episcopacy is not essentially sacramental in basis, so it is not diocesan in structure. The clergy of an annual conference are members of an itinerant order of preachers, not extensions of the bishop's ministry as in diocesan ecclesiology. Church members within the bounds of an annual conference are members of the UM connection and of a local church, not members of a bishop's extended parish (to which he confirms the new members) as in a diocese.

UM episcopacy is definitely more regionalized than its predecessors, but to call it thereby diocesan distracts UM people from the real issues. Limitation of the jurisdiction of bishops has coincided with a vast increase in the size and scale of annual conferences. With the recent trend toward merger of annual conferences within civil states (Arkansas, Illinois, Kentucky, Mississippi, Missouri, and New Jersey, with others to follow) the number of conferences in the United States has dropped under sixty-five while the number of bishops in the United States stands at fifty.[9] Annual conferences have become regional entities with assemblies of thousands, numerous program and administrative employees, and structures for oversight of multiple institutions and missions. Their elders are ordained into the itinerant ministry of the connection, but in practice most give their careers to service within the regional "chapter" of their order. In sum, the regionalization of episcopacy follows from a broader trend toward regionalization of the UM connection in the U.S.

One concrete way in which bishops have continued to practice their general oversight is through their service as presidents and members of the General Conference agencies for connectional ministry. But this has raised a second issue about the scope of episcopal authority. The bishops are not executives or staff members of agencies, many of whom serve longer terms than the bishops. Nor do the bishops have standing as agency members distinguishable from other clergy or laity, except for the tradition of electing a bishop to preside. This particular form of general oversight has proved limited, then. The bishops may bring extraordinary gifts of connectional experience and knowledge to their general agency roles, but they are not formally set apart from other members by their episcopal status.

For the last generation at least, the bishops have been seeking ways to enhance their general oversight through their own Council. They have tried to put their remarkably comprehensive overview of the whole connection into practical forms. They have advanced several episcopal initiatives as a Council, issued major teaching statements to the Church, and invited a broad range of representatives of connectional ministries to report to them. They have explored social and theological issues. They took on the stymied General Conference ordained ministry studies of 1988 and 1992 and brought a report to the 1996 General Conference, in contradiction to the historic separation of episcopacy from legislative powers. They have worked toward Christian unity and interreligious understanding, continuing the tradition of bishops leading the churches in ecumenical conversations and church unions.[10]

Nonetheless, a survey of the practice of "general" *episkopē* in United Methodism shows that it is widely shared among conferences and councils, not limited to the bishops. If one were to argue that it comes to particular representation and focus in the bishops' role, one would be hard-pressed to say exactly how that representation results in actions really distinctive for Church life. United Methodism, like The Methodist Church and other predecessor bodies, does not include "Episcopal" in its name nor grant its bishops the full range of general *episkopē*. Any proposals for significant change in this arrangement will run headlong into the same populism and democratic instinct that created a widely dispersed *episkopē* in the first place.

Episkopē as Superintending

When Wesley named the oversight function for the Methodist connection, he chose the translation of *episkopos* common among Lutheran and Reformed churches beginning in the sixteenth century Reformation. Refusing the hierarchical overtones of the term "bishop," these traditions adopted a term of Latin root, superintendent. While the term included roles of super-vision—over-seeing an endeavor—super-intendency more broadly meant the focused extension or assertion of a purpose. It suggested directing one's thoughts or turning one's attention (intend) to the whole (super). The heart of superintendency was the intentional fulfillment of the Church's ministry and mission. For Methodism this has meant an office of superintendent with a central purpose of attending to the Church's direction through the work of its conferences and ministers.

The core roles of superintendency—presiding over conferences and appointing clergy to their places—have always been the domain of Methodist bishops and to a great extent have remained so. While there is provision for a conference to elect an elder to preside in the absence of a bishop, everyone expects and counts on bishops to have the chair. So strong is the UM confidence in this presiding role and its necessity for the well-being of the Church that the 2004 committee planning General Conference has proposed that bishops preside over legislative committees for the first time. In every form of conference, UM people trust that having a bishop preside will free the body from political bias in the chair. The bishops' separation from legislative powers and lack of voice in the body, together with the bishops' presidential powers to enforce the body's own rules of procedure, creates a space in which voices may be freely heard and the balance of opinion and collective wisdom can be openly sought.

The bishops' superintendency expressed through appointive powers has also remained essentially intact, though much modified through the many social and ecclesiological changes of recent generations. The *Discipline* still charges the bishop "to make and fix the appointments in the annual conferences" (¶ 416.1), but the autocratic power of an individual bishop to appoint pastors, so much a part of the lore of the past, has given way to a far more consultative process. The paragraphs on consultation, added in 1976 as part of the General Conference study of ministry and episcopacy, broadened the *episkopē* of appointive powers to include the voice of the local church, the pastor, and the district super-intendent. While practices vary among the bishops, depending on each one's interpretation of the paragraphs, the *Discipline* does call for a full, detailed effort to match ministerial gifts with congregational mission. Unlike the insistent itinerancy of earlier generations, in which a strict limit of four years in one place was assumed, today's *Discipline* encourages longer tenures and thus more intentionality about creating strong and lasting matches (¶ 434).

District superintendency has also continued to emerge more definitely as an office of *episkopē* in the Church. Bishops appoint the district super-intendents, thus extending and further localizing episcopal powers and duties through the two offices. Just as bishops have their ecclesiological standing as members of the Council of Bishops, so the *Discipline* assigns the district superintendents to their own conciliar body, the cabinet, as the locus of their office of superintendency. District superintendents share fully in the appointment process, as bishops depend heavily on them for the local knowledge that will make for good appointments. District superintendents also share in the office of presidency by presid-ing over district and charge conferences, and they exercise oversight of the ministry and mission of their districts. Like the bishops, district super-intendents travel constantly through their districts and are present at most annual conference events. They represent the unity of the connec-tion more locally and in some ways more vividly and immediately than the bishops.

The consistency of these superintending roles over time may actually reinforce the regionalization trends explored earlier. That is, since pre-siding and appointing have continued to be expressions of *episkopē* clearly identified with bishops, and since these roles are carried out mainly within the annual conference(s) of the bishop's residence, extended by district superintendents whom the bishop appoints from among the elders of the conference, the roles have made episcopacy more local in practice. From a different perspective, though, the conciliar form of *episkopē* in a cabinet can be viewed as spreading the oversight function more evenly and consistently across the whole connection. The more local extension of *episkopē* through district superintendency is insepara-ble from its more global reach through general superintendency. A global connection has no meaning apart from its local expressions, and local mission is vastly deepened and enlivened by connection with the min-istries of the whole Church in the world.

Back to "the Plan"

The UM constitution protects "the plan of itinerant general superintendency" as it has done since 1808. Yet a survey of these two hundred years and of current practice shows that the Church has continually reformed and broadened oversight—the functions of *episkopē*—to give a variety of conferences and councils an episcopal role. This wider *episkopē* is in the service of the Church's mission, in fact has been extended specifically in order to enable the Church better to fulfill its mission.

The question now is what plan for bishops today can best enhance their role as *episkopoi*, bringing to focus the functions of oversight in the Church. How could their constitutional powers and duties better serve the Church's mission? To this we turn in part 2.

Notes

1. Ephraim Radner, "Bad Bishops: A Key to Anglican Ecclesiology," *Anglican Theological Review* 82, no. 2 (Spring 2000): 321-42.

2. Jack M. Tuell, "The United Methodist Bishop and *The Book of Discipline*" in Tuell and Fjeld, eds., *Episcopacy: Lutheran-United Methodist Dialogue II* (Minneapolis: Augsburg, 1991), p. 76.

3. On the relationship of bishops and presbyters in the early church and the significance of eucharistic presidency in defining these offices, see Alvin F. Kimel Jr., "Who Are the Bishops? *Episkopē* and the Church," *Anglican Theological Review* 77, no. 1 (Winter 1995): 58-76. Kimel argues that even in Anglicanism, the bishop's role as "regional administrator" divorces the bishop too much from "eucharistic identity" in the gathered congregation.

4. For discussion of this distinction in the New Testament, see Raymond E. Brown, "*Episkopē* and *Episkopos*: The New Testament Evidence," *Theological Studies* 41, no. 2 (June 1980): 322-38.

5. James Mathews, *Set Apart to Serve: The Meaning and Role of Episcopacy in the Wesleyan Tradition* (Nashville: Abingdon Press, 1985), pp. 206-7.

6. Ibid., p. 207.

7. Murray H. Leiffer, *The Episcopacy in the Present Day* (Evanston, Ill.: Bureau of Social and Religious Research, 1963), pp. 147-48.

8. James E. Kirby, *The Episcopacy in American Methodism* (Nashville: Abingdon Press/Kingswood, 2000), p. 242.

9. In 1960 The Methodist Church in the United States had ninety-four annual conferences presided over by less than forty bishops. At the time of merger in 1968, the much smaller EUBC had thirty-two conferences and seven active bishops.

10. For a summary of the bishops' role in church unions, see Roy H. Short, *The Episcopal Leadership Role in United Methdodism* (Nashville: Abingdon Press, 1985), pp. 17-47.

PART TWO

Proposals

Frank

Should Bishops Be Elected at General Conference?

The aspirations that the bishops have for the Council and its leadership invite our consideration of where and how we elect bishops. We propose that the UMC look seriously at returning episcopal elections to the General Conference, their original locus. While this proposal would be complex to implement, we suggest that the denomination has reached a point in its evolution toward a global community where episcopal elections at General Conference might greatly help the Church achieve its missional purpose. In this first thought experiment, we explore the constitutional and practical issues to be weighed and alternative scenarios, and encourage the denomination to work through the issues involved on behalf of an invigorated general superintendency. Our proposal will reinforce "the plan" of episcopacy, showing the fullness of the bishops' service on behalf of the whole Church—a reflection of Christ's office of servanthood.

Jurisdictional conference powers and duties are derivative of General

Conference. Everything that jurisdictional conferences do originally was done in General Conference, which in 1939 delegated to jurisdictions certain powers for episcopal elections, general agency nominations, and oversight of Church institutions. All delegates who collectively consti-tute General Conference also constitute jurisdictional conferences, together with an equal number of additional delegates. Jurisdictional con-ferences are a kind of regional continuation and expansion of General Conference, with the election of bishops their primary power.

Central conferences have a distinct origin in the needs of United Methodist churches of various nations other than the United States. They have made possible a *Discipline* adapted to the regional culture of each place, and thereby better able to sustain ministry and mission that is embedded in the language, customs, and social trends of indigenous peoples. While these conferences were served for several generations by bishops from the United States (most of whom were elected in General Conference), since the 1960s they have elected their bishops from among their own clergy.

Rationales

Many voices across the UMC, particularly in the United States, have argued that the election of bishops in regional conferences abrogates the "plan of itinerant general superintendency" protected by the constitu-tion. That is, if bishops are elected in a region, and if their "residential and presidential supervision" is restricted to that region only, in what sense can the Church maintain the myth that bishops are general super-intendents or bishops of the whole Church? Individual bishops carry out their general church duties through membership of general agencies, vis-itations of conferences in parts of the world other than their own, and participation in the COB. But their primary responsibilities lie in the region in which they were elected.

Many people have advocated returning the election of bishops to General Conference as a way of reestablishing the general oversight of all bishops. Election in the delegate assembly of world United Methodism would give individual bishops a more global base for their superinten-dency. As the COB came over time to be comprised of bishops elected by General Conference, the Council itself would be more clearly established as the conciliar body of episcopal oversight for the whole connection. Since general oversight belongs first to the COB, not to individual bishops, election of bishops by a worldwide assembly would give that conciliar oversight genuine substance and authority.

Others argue that such a change would tilt the balance of episcopal oversight too much toward the general and away from the local. Regional elections are necessary, these voices insist, to the well-being of the Church in each place. Central conferences need to be able to elect bishops with the background and language skills to practice superintendency in a complex multicultural environment, since episcopal areas are often comprised of annual conferences in distinct nations. Jurisdictional conferences need to be assured of being able to elect bishops from their respective region in order to keep the COB balanced across the varied subcultures of the United States.

Individual bishops understandably feel a primary allegiance and accountability to the conference that elected them. Bishops do not routinely move from one jurisdiction to another in the United States. And it is highly unusual to elect a bishop from outside the jurisdiction. The delegates of the conference that elected a bishop continue to be a community of affinity and support as the bishop practices her episcopacy. Moving the elections to General Conference would tend to move that mutual loyalty from the regional to the global Church. A bishop might find it more difficult to identify any specific community of support in a connection as far-flung and diverse as the UMC.

Episcopal Candidacies

A General Conference election would require much more effort to circulate information and create venues through which delegates could get acquainted with possible candidates for bishop. Almost all annual conferences consider their first-elected clergy delegate for General Conference to be their nominee for the episcopacy. Thus their delegate elections become a kind of nomination process that reflects the conference's knowledge of a candidate and advocacy of his or her gifts for episcopacy. Each conference then seeks ways to inform other annual conferences about the candidate during the year leading up to jurisdictional conference. If all annual conferences in the world participated in such a process, some means for delegates to be informed about all of the approximately ninety candidates would be absolutely essential.

Since elections are not limited to nominees, of course, other persons could receive votes and possibly be elected. At General Conference this would likely mean that persons relatively better known across the connection, such as seminary presidents or general secretaries of agencies, would receive votes. The chances of the Spirit moving the body toward consensus around a person not as well-known, or possibly not even nominated or suggested prior to conference, would seem more remote in a general church assembly.

A General Conference election might also stir annual conferences to put forward nominees who are better known across the connection already. This might run counter to the widely noted trends in who gets elected bishop in the jurisdictional conferences of the UMC. As Dennis Campbell argued, "Bishops tend to be alike because most have taken the same path to get elected."[1] Of the 123 bishops elected from 1972 through 2001 (including the first-ever special session of a jurisdiction, the Southeastern, convened in 2001 to replace a deceased bishop), 103 were serving as local church pastors, district superintendents, or annual conference administrators at the time of their election.[2] Since transfers between annual conferences are relatively rare, this means that most bishops have served their entire careers within the bounds of their particular conference and their nomination for bishop comes at least in part in recognition of their service and seniority within the conference. Most have also served as General Conference delegates before, and thus as members of general agencies and boards of institutions. But their career experience does not necessarily include the skills in personnel administration, finance, and governance that a bishop often finds essential to her work.

The larger question of General Conference elections is whether they would result in the election of persons with the best kind of "proven experience (a specific track record) at doing the kinds of things a bishop must do."[3] The annual conference nomination process may not be the best way to achieve this. Within jurisdictions, the process tends to emphasize what Campbell called annual conference chauvinism, with ballot blocks being traded back and forth and conferences with larger delegations dominating.[4] General Conference elections might break this dynamic down, of course, since power would be more widely dispersed in a body of 1,000 delegates.

More broadly, because of its global diversity, General Conference would have to establish a process for putting forward the names of any individuals for whom any group wanted to express support, perhaps through a biography of everyone who receives votes on the first ballot.

Such information, distributed in the multiple languages of a global Church, would be absolutely essential if elections were to transcend mere trading off of voting blocks. Perhaps most challenging of all, U.S. delegates would have to be willing and committed to learning the UMC of other nations and their candidates for bishop. The less information delegates have, the more susceptible they would be to the influences of ideological camps and political power brokers.

The inclusiveness and diversity of episcopal elections is at stake in any reform plan. A global body might not have the same intentionality about achieving greater ethnic and gender balance in the United States that jurisdictions have. In 2000–2001 the jurisdictions elected fourteen bishops, including seven white men, four black men, and three black women. Whether or not this indicates a trend, it does show a degree of awareness of diversity issues in U.S. society that might not be as apparent to General Conference delegates from outside the United States who now comprise 15 percent of the conference. (Of course, intentionality about diversity is not uniform across the United States; the Southeastern Jurisdiction has elected only one woman in its history.)

Alternatives

One possible alternative to a General Conference election would be for the UMC in the United States to become a central conference itself. This plan would recognize the United States as one nation among others, rather than as the dominant force in the UMC. Constituting the United States as a central conference would acknowledge that the nation is just as diverse, multicultural, and multilingual as many other nations of the world and that the Church's ministry and mission must be equally supple and adaptable.

Elections for all U.S. bishops could then occur in a session of the U.S. central conference at the site of General Conference, which for the foreseeable future will meet in the United States. Some formula for ensuring regional balance in the elections would prevent the U.S. regions with the most delegates from electing all the bishops. Elections of bishops for nations other than the United States could continue in their respective central conferences, meeting in the same year as General Conference at a site within their bounds.

Yet another alternative would call for all jurisdictional conferences to meet at the site of General Conference, elect their bishops, and then consecrate them all together in a General Conference rite. This could become a grand symbolic endorsement of general superintendency, and save the costs of two separate conference sessions for the General Conference delegations. This plan would exclude the central conferences, however, which would still have to meet and elect bishops in their own regions. They could hold their elections before General Conference meets and send their electees for consecration. But far fewer central conference representatives would be able to participate in the ritual. Such arrangements might reinforce the long-standing dynamic of U.S. bishops dominating the COB as the "real" general superintendents of the denomination.

Jurisdictional conference elections either at regional sites or at the site of General Conference would enable the present system of episcopal assignments to continue. Election of bishops by General Conference, or in a new U.S. central conference, would require a new process for assignment. Presumably the persons elected would have to be willing to go wherever in the world, or in the United States, they are asked to go. A constitutional amendment deleting the restriction of episcopal supervision to jurisdictional boundaries would be necessary. An assignment committee would have the challenging task of placing bishops based on sound information about the diverse places of ministry in global United Methodism.

A reform in the opposite direction might also be possible. As the UMC in the United States moves increasingly toward the arrangement of each bishop presiding over one annual conference, a suggestion of episcopal elections by annual conferences may surface. This could parallel the process in the Protestant Episcopal Church, in which a diocese receives nominations from inside and outside its bounds, examines candidates, puts forward a limited number of names for a ballot, and elects its bishop in a delegate assembly representing all parishes in the diocese. The Episcopalians have a relatively stronger ecclesiology of bishops focused in a theology of the diocese as an extended parish and the bishop as chief sacramental officer. This counteracts the localizing tendency of diocesan election, since the bishop has broader ecclesiological standing within the tradition.

Lacking such a theology, United Methodists would have to find other ways to establish the more general authority of a bishop in spite of her or his being elected in an annual conference to preside over that conference. The constitutional powers of the COB could be greatly widened and strengthened to include a legislative role, for example, with the bishops functioning as a second legislative house in General Conference. The bishops could still itinerate as well, after a mandatory period of service with the conference that elected them. A General Conference equivalent of the jurisdictional committee on episcopacy would review their work, appraise their gifts, and assign them to appropriate presidencies of annual conferences that preferred receiving an experienced bishop to electing a new one.

The Theology of Episcopacy

Electing bishops within General Conference, the body that alone is and has been empowered to speak for the Church, would not in itself oblige the Church to be theologically more self-conscious about the office. After all, the churches that now constitute United Methodism selected leadership at the general level before the unions of 1939 and 1968. And the predecessor churches had not sustained a rich and vibrant tradition of theological reflection about episcopacy. We cannot return to those periods to pick up the theological agenda. Indeed, as our above excursions into earlier history were designed to indicate, Methodism has really never had a theology of the office in any way approximate to its rich intellectual, biblical, and missional potential. Bishops Coke and Asbury made a remarkable start in their annotated *Discipline* of 1798 but neither they nor others sustained theologizing about episcopacy at that level thereafter.

Election at the general level would, we think, make bishops symbolically "itinerant general superintendents," would encourage the delegates to think about the general needs of the Church in their balloting and in their conception of the office, might elicit candidacies whose experience and talents have already been tested on a churchwide basis, would make more thinkable appointment on a connectional basis, and in a variety of ways could enhance the cross-fertilization that broader episcopal deployment and exchanges permit.

Those practicalities, again, in and of themselves, do not guarantee that we would reflect more deeply about the office. However, reflecting on effective Christian practices has been our tradition. This practical theology or theology of practice, modeled by John and Charles Wesley, we now recognize as a powerful way of sustaining our fidelity to the Scripture. The practice of electing at the general level would, we think, stimulate our theologizing about episcopacy. It would make it possible for us to think hard about itinerant general superintendency, to do so mindful of other understandings of *episkopē*, to draw together conceptually what has been achieved programmatically within the Council of Bishops, and to develop a distinctively Methodist theology of the office.

Certainly in such reflection we should underscore the connectional "service" that the bishops individually and collectively have committed themselves to in their various episcopal initiatives, most dramatically in that on children and poverty. We can do even more conceptually with respect to episcopacy, as for ministry and ecclesiology generally, with service as one of the four basic ministerial rubrics. It offers great christological potential. It is not sufficient, however, to point to him who models our leadership, Christ the suffering servant, and then load in current notions of servant leadership drawn from handbooks for corporate America.

Furthermore, putting service alongside Word, Sacrament, and order, if that quadrilateral is to be sustained theologically, requires us to take on the long Christian tradition of reflecting on Christ's three offices of prophet (Word), priest (Sacrament), and king (Order). The fourfold rather than threefold office—of Christ and of his ministry today—may be a more faithful reading of the Scripture than that practiced for 2,000 years. One might argue that Coke and Asbury indeed thought so. They read our plan of itinerant general superintendency as a leap back to the primitive Church to recover an apostolic and missional understanding of the office. They demonstrated to their own satisfaction that the apostles functioned itinerantly and generally, that that was the scriptural pattern of leadership. They did not reflect systematically and christologically on such service in relation to prophetic, priestly, and royal roles. That may be a place for us to start. At the very least, we can make use of their efforts.

And, if we decide to think practically and theologically about election at the general level, we should evoke memories of Francis Asbury's dramatic initiative in demanding the convening of a general conference of the preachers in 1784 to exercise an elective role in the selection of bishops for the Church. His initiative established the necessity thereafter of such a general gathering for episcopal elections. By making bishops clearly servants of the entire Church, this proposal corresponds, we suggest, with his plan—"the plan" part of our "plan of our itinerant general superintendency."

Notes

1. Dennis M. Campbell, "Is There a Better Way to Elect Bishops?" in Russell E. Richey, William B. Lawrence, and Dennis M. Campbell, eds., *Questions for the Twenty-first Century Church* (Nashville: Abingdon Press, 1999), pp. 186-93. Quotation from p. 93.

2. Data expanded from Craig This, "Who Gets Elected Bishop in The United Methodist Church?" Unpublished paper. November 1997.

3. Campbell, "Better Way," p. 193.

4. Ibid., pp. 189-90.

PROPOSAL 2

Constitutional Issues of a Council of Bishops Presidency

In November 2002, the Council of Bishops adopted a proposal for a bishop to serve as president of the Council for a four-year term without residential responsibilities in an episcopal area. The Judicial Council ruled in April 2003 that the proposal requires a constitutional amendment. We propose that the UMC act to create a Council presidency. While some may fear that such an office will reinforce hierarchy, we argue that if practiced in a pastoral form growing out of a sacramental theology, the office will make the Council of Bishops far more effective. A Council presidency will enhance the itinerant general superintendency by giving it a conciliar substance and consistency that it has lacked. It will make it more possible for the bishops to exercise their constitutional duties of conciliar oversight, by giving them a continuing organization for their work. Our proposal is an expression of Methodism's unique episcopacy as it reinforces the itinerancy or constant travel and presence of the Council's president, and expresses the ministry of Sacrament—Christ's priestly office.

The proposal for a Council presidency raises some intriguing constitutional issues for the UMC. Some might dismiss such issues as minutiae of church law. But the constitution names, constitutes, and brings into being, the elements that create the UMC. The constitution is comprised of those principles and entities of the denomination that make it what it is. To put it conversely, to remove or significantly alter these elements would change the nature of the denomination. Constitutional issues are at the heart of how the denomination conceives and carries out its ministry and mission, and are fundamental to the future of the denomination.

What the bishops propose would mark a shift in the balance of powers of the UMC constitution and a major new initiative in how the episcopal role is practiced. In brief, the proposal calls for a president to be elected by the Council itself for a four-year term, during which the president would not have responsibility for residential and presidential supervision of an episcopal area. He or she would give full time to the activities of the Council and its presidency, serving as the chief ecumenical officer for the denomination and liaison between the Council and the various agencies of General Conference. The presidential office would constitute the first role of its kind for the Council, including a small staff and actual place of business. Heretofore, the Council has had only a half-time support staff person to coordinate their semiannual meetings, and a General Council on Finance and Administration staff person to service episcopal salary, insurance, and other Episcopal Fund matters. The Council has never had an actual office suite or address for itself as a conciliar entity.

The 2002 proposal is the fruit of a conversation that has continued for some years. Many bishops and students of the episcopal role in the Church have noted the contemporary complexity of oversight, including growth in the size of the Council and the scope of what it undertakes. Increasing recognition of the global nature of the Church, along with a desire for the bishops to take more conciliar initiative on issues facing the Church, have led many to suggest a more formal, continuing support structure and a visible, substantive office of presidency. Even the 1960–1964 study of the episcopacy in The Methodist Church floated the possibility of a presidency. That study did eventuate in legislation adopted by the 1964 General Conference to permit the Council to assign one of its own members for a special mission for a year, with possible extension to two years. This provision gave the Council greater flexibility for taking conciliar initiative in matters of concern to the Church as a whole, though it was not utilized for twenty-five years. The next General

Conference (1968) sent a constitutional amendment authorizing a Council presidency to the annual conferences, where it was approved. But when it returned to the 1970 General Conference for a final vote (a reversal of the usual process), it was defeated.

Judicial Council Ruling

The Council forwarded its 2002 proposal to the Judicial Council for a declaratory decision—a ruling on whether such legislation would be constitutional were it to be adopted by General Conference. In April 2003, the Judicial Council issued its decision (No. 961). Staying close to the language of the division on "Episcopal Supervision" in the constitution, the Council gave a narrow interpretation of ¶ 47. "The bishops shall have residential and presidential supervision in the jurisdictional or central conferences in which they are elected or to which they are transferred" means, the Council stated, that all bishops must carry "residential and presidential responsibilities." A presidency of the Council of Bishops that entailed no such responsibilities is not contemplated by the constitution. A constitutional amendment would be necessary.

The brief filed by the Council of Bishops in this case argued that since ¶ 47 did not explicitly say "each bishop shall," the paragraph was placing in the hands of the bishops a collective responsibility for providing residential and presidential supervision as they saw fit. If the bishops decided to include a form of service other than residential and presidential supervision, that was their collective prerogative. This latitude of authority was reinforced by the immediately preceding paragraph (¶ 46), which charges each jurisdictional or central conference College of Bishops to "arrange the plan of episcopal supervision of the annual conferences."

The Judicial Council obviously did not take the bishops' point. The Council's decision was based on the Church's common reading of the constitution, under which all bishops do carry "residential and presidential responsibilities." Under the provisions of ¶ 48, each bishop receives an assignment to an episcopal area as proposed by the jurisdictional committee on episcopacy and approved by the jurisdictional or central conference. The bishops' brief suggested a parallel between their presidency proposal and the provision for special assignments, a connection that the Judicial Council apparently did not find. The legislative paragraph added in 1964 and still in effect in the 2000 *Discipline* (¶ 407.3) allows for a bishop to receive a special assignment "to some specific churchwide responsibility" for a year, renewable for a second year. The paragraph calls for the Council to assign another bishop, active or retired, to fulfill the absent bishop's residential and presidential responsibilities. The special assignment is arranged as a kind of leave from regular duties, with the bishop returning to the area upon its completion. The jurisdictional or central conference committee on episcopacy has to concur in the Council's decision to make a special assignment. This provision has been used only once in forty years, when Bishop Felton May focused the Church's attention on at-risk urban neighborhoods during his assignment in 1989–1990.

The bishops' brief suggested that the special assignment provision had never been challenged constitutionally because it was a constitutional prerogative of the Council of Bishops. Under the second full paragraph of ¶ 47, they argued, the Council could assign one of its members "for presidential service or other temporary service in another jurisdiction than that which elected the bishop." A special assignment, they deduced, must count as "temporary service." But the intentions of that provision in ¶ 47 are exceedingly difficult to interpret. Since the jurisdictional committee on episcopacy does not have to be consulted or concur, the provision seems parallel with the next paragraph authorizing the Council to assign a bishop across jurisdictional lines in case of an emergency need to cover for a bishop on leave or absent because of illness, death, or other causes. This, too, never happens since jurisdictional Colleges of Bishops view themselves as exclusively responsible for the territory of their jurisdiction.

Contradictory Constitutional Intentions

The basic intent of ¶ 47 as a whole is to establish the jurisdictional scope of authority for bishops, and to provide ways in which episcopal authority can cross jurisdictional lines. These are contradictory intentions imbedded in the history of this constitution. Episcopal authority was made jurisdictional in 1939 for two basic reasons: to preserve the regional character particularly of southern Methodism, and to ensure that white and black bishops would not have authority to preside in each other's jurisdictions (the Central Jurisdiction being Methodism's apartheid system of the time). At the same time, jurisdictions clearly marked a new limitation in the Church's general superintendency, and provision was made to counteract too strong a regionalization of the

Church by setting up a procedure through which bishops could transfer between jurisdictions or serve in a jurisdiction other than the one in which they were elected. None of these procedures have ever been used. Even Bishop May served his special assignment within the bounds of his own jurisdiction.

Since the bishops' presidential proposal has to do with their conciliar oversight of the general church, the constitution's paragraphs on jurisdictional authority do not provide the appropriate warrant. Both ¶ 46 and ¶ 47 give the bishops wide scope of authority to plan for episcopal supervision, but always within jurisdictional lines. Some other constitutional warrant for a "special assignment" would seem to be a more promising basis for assignment of a Council president. But what is that warrant? Overall, the constitution is so minimalist in its approach to episcopacy that one is hard-pressed to find a basis even for the retirement of bishops. They are granted life tenure (¶ 48), but nothing is said about their right to "cease to travel," in the historic language. Both retirement and the provisions for various kinds of leaves added in 1976 (¶¶ 409, 411) have to be interpreted as not touching the constitutional foundations of episcopacy, but as episcopal assignments made by the jurisdictional conference in parallel with the listing of clergy on leave or retired in an annual conference. This reasoning may stand in contradiction to the Judicial Council's decision that ¶ 47 requires that "each bishop shall have residential and presidential responsibilities," since bishops on leave or retired obviously do not.

Trumping Paragraph 45?

The constitutional warrant for the bishops as general superintendents in Council to provide for their oversight of the whole Church clearly lies in ¶ 45. No jurisdictional limitation of powers is named here. One could infer that since the Council is authorized only to *plan* for its "general oversight and promotion of the temporal and spiritual interests of the entire Church" (italics ours), the constitution intends for this oversight to be carried out jurisdictionally. But the paragraph certainly does not have to be read that way.

The warrant of conciliar general oversight is the only definite, if broad, constitutional basis for any episcopal assignment other than residential and presidential supervision within a jurisdiction. The bishops' brief suggested in an aside that "a plausible case can be made that the Council of

Bishops already possesses the authority to make such an assignment [of a president] without any new legislation," but that it was "more appropriate . . . to seek the explicit authorization of the General Conference." This claim finds its only grounds in ¶ 45 (not in the second paragraph of ¶ 47, as the brief argues).

This puts us at the nub of the constitutional balance of powers. Do the bishops have authority to carry out their general oversight as a conciliar body without seeking authorization from General Conference for particular means of carrying out their mandate? Or are the bishops agents of General Conference and amenable to it for the conciliar conduct of their office?

The proposal for a four-year presidency of the Council without other episcopal responsibilities brings these constitutional questions to a head. The Judicial Council argued that the bishop's proposal "effects a fundamental change in the contours and content of the plan of the Church's itinerant general superintendency," which is specifically governed by ¶ 47. Jurisdictional authority in that sense puts the broad powers that appear to be granted in ¶ 45 into a more limited framework, mandating that every bishop in Council also have an assignment to an episcopal area. Powers of general oversight are practiced in Council by bishops who also have specific regional supervisory responsibilities. No conciliar oversight is practiced apart from such regional assignments.

We argue that the Judicial Council has advanced too narrow an interpretation of the constitution. Its ruling allows a strict reading of ¶ 47 to trump the broad authorization of ¶ 45. Their decision suggests that there are no substantively conciliar episcopal powers that can realistically be enabled apart from the powers of bishops for residential and presidential supervision in a jurisdiction or central conference. The bishops in Council are a collection of individuals who can make joint statements or take limited collective actions in occasional meetings but whose primary episcopacy is practiced within their jurisdictional assignment.

Recovering *Episkopē*

We maintain that the Church needs to move beyond the cautions and restraints of the jurisdictional system and realize the full breadth of the constitution's authorization of general oversight through the Council of Bishops. To do so will require cutting new channels for at least two traditional streams of practice in Methodist episcopacy. One is the fierce individualism and independence of the bishops that was exemplified in Asbury, McKendree, Soule, and others. For years the bishops did not meet regularly, and then only to agree on their own schedules for presiding over annual conferences. As recently as 1976, Bishop Roy Short could generalize that "no Methodist bishop is bound even by any action of the bishops meeting in council, except as he chooses so to be."[1] Only after the area system was firmly in place did bishops agree to go where sent by their jurisdictions. Even now the *Discipline* attempts no constitutional or legislative language to define what an episcopal area actually is, surely an echo of the historic autonomy of bishops to plan their own supervisory duties.

The second traditional stream is the steady dispersion of *episkopē* among a number of conciliar and conference bodies over the past century, to the extent that the conciliar episcopacy of bishops has been rendered nominal. The Council of Bishops has had no forms of oversight specifically legislated in the *Discipline*. This again might be considered a way to honor the bishops' collective autonomy. But in practice the lack of specificity has meant that the Council has no effective role in oversight of the agencies of General Conference, for example, and limited opportunity to move the ministry and mission of the Church in new directions. Most oversight and initiative in the general church has belonged to the laity and clergy that comprise the membership of agencies, and to the agency staff.

Any fuller realization of general oversight by the Council of Bishops must harness the autonomy of bishops to the Church's need for oversight that has substance and consistency. The bishops must deepen their allegiance to their own conciliar body and individually honor their collective actions. The Church must assign some of the widely dispersed responsibilities of *episkopē* to the Council of Bishops.

A full-time four-year presidency of the Council of Bishops would enhance this invigorated conciliar oversight. It would allow one bishop to give full attention to the Council's responsibilities and to organize the work of recently retired bishops in specific areas of need. It would give the Council an office and staff to support its initiatives. It would put in place a structure through which the Council could take on specific duties of oversight assigned by General Conference.

The bishops' constitutional powers would be greatly enhanced through a conciliar structure with a president. A radical construal of these powers, drawing on the southern church's (Methodist Episcopal Church South) tradition of episcopacy being a constitutional entity coequal with General Conference, would argue for the bishops simply electing their own Council president (based on ¶ 45) and informing the appropriate jurisdictional committee on episcopacy that he or she is not available for assignment (based on ¶ 46). But since such an action would require cooperation among many different bodies (coordination of how many bishops a jurisdictional conference needs to elect, for example), such autonomous action is not realistic.

A more constructive construal of these powers would have the bishops propose the necessary constitutional amendment to authorize a presidency. A simple sentence could be added to the end of ¶ 45:

> The Council of Bishops may elect a president from among the active members of the Council, to serve a four-year term with such duties as the Council may determine, with release from residential and presidential responsibilities during that term.

This preserves the autonomy of the bishops to fulfill their general oversight by electing their own president and determining the duties of the office. Enabling legislation would be added to the chapter on episcopacy, describing procedures for matters such as rotating the presidency among various jurisdictions and central conferences so that they can plan episcopal elections and assignments.

A yet more moderate version of the proposal would have the General Conference authorize the job description in the enabling legislation, or even elect the president from among nominees provided by the Council. This would bring the proposal more fully back into the sway of General Conference powers, making the post amenable to General Conference and to the Council itself. But the Council would still have some capacities for oversight that it currently lacks.

A Theology of Itinerant Presidency

A decision that a more permanent presidency of the Council is appropriate, constructive, and important will offer the Church ample opportunity to reflect theologically on our episcopacy. Indeed, one might argue that the Church ought to start there. The theological case for a president could be advanced before the Church made efforts to test the issue politically, or to explore it operationally, or to advance constitutional arguments or remedies.

What might such a presidency mean for our understanding—our theology—of episcopacy, for the *episkopē* of individual bishops as also for the Council, for the district superintendency, for the relation of bishops and Council to General Conference, for the authority to speak for the Church, and for the exercise of the teaching office? The Council could indeed acquire administrative leadership in this pattern but should that be the primary concern? Or if that is the primary concern, is "president" the right term for such an administrative role? Would a re-envisioned Council secretary be more in keeping with responsibilities so delimited?

On the presumption that "presidency" is the right term, we suggest that it should be thought about in the fullest and most theological fashion. Administration in the ordinary or conventional sense of that word may be needed. Presidency could entail that and much more. We could and perhaps should be thinking theologically about the office and administration, accenting the rich sacramental nuances of presidency. A sacramentally understood presidency—a presidency in the first instance at the table and baptismal font—would permit the Council what it needs for its efficient operation but robe efficiencies in the garb of the episcopal office itself. A Council president could be an itinerant priest, a sign of the Church's concern for the world (general), a superintendent whose model is Christ.

Understood in this priestly, sacramental fashion, but as an itinerant rather than in either executive or archdiocesan terms, the president would stand for the denomination's and the Council's missional orientation. What the Council and the Church need for ministries to the world seems to be, in fact, the underlying concern in the bishops' proposal. We need, appropriately then, a conception of the office oriented to the church's priestly responsibilities, to those that ministers generally exercise and then to those that we might expect and need from our bishops individually, in Council, and in such a special leadership role. We should, therefore, think of a president less in terms of the modern corporation's CEO or the U.S. presidency than in relation to Christ's priestly office.

It might indeed be fitting that the Council have a president and that the president be thought of as our chief sacramental officer. He or she would itinerate across the Church, as did Francis Asbury, the Church's first chief priest. This initiative or proposal seemingly would do less, perhaps, than the following two to enhance the "itinerant general superintendency"

125

of all the bishops (though the election of all in general conference and their appointment across the connection rather than regionally would decidedly improve on the present diocesan deployment). It might seem that United Methodism's *episkopē* would all be focused in this one office. However, understanding the president's office as sacramental in character might, in fact, do less to erode the stature and "itinerant general" role of individual bishops than a presidency charged primarily with the Council's operations. Indeed, a president who led out of his or her sacramental responsibilities might exercise other roles and relate to other bishops in such a way as to enhance and enlarge rather than further erode their itinerant general sacramental character. Certainly that was true for those around Asbury. In his general itinerancy and exercise of his priestly leadership roles he pulled others with him. While he itinerated nationally so did presiding elders and preachers. And a president so understood might similarly pose less operational or constitutional challenge to General Conference's right to speak for the Church.

Should the Church decide to permit or encourage a "set-aside" presiding bishop for the Council, it can perhaps get some help theologically and practically from other communions with similar offices, in particular the Episcopal Church. Another theological resource, to be found in various ecumenical treatises and richly nuanced, is in discussions of ministry as representative. United Methodism might wish to restore the Disciplinary language on representation excised by the 1996 General Conference. "Representation" nicely captures the *sacramental* dimensions of the office so conceived and so authorized. The president of the Council could, indeed, be present for United Methodism and for the Council in those places requiring ceremonial or official representation.

A similarly excised treatment, the Journey of a Connectional People, could possibly be of help. The *Disciplines* for 1988 and 1992 carried an eloquent section entitled "The Journey of a Connectional People." It spoke of connection as shared vision, memory, community, discipline, leadership, mobilization, and linkage.[2] Such language might be drawn upon in conceptualizing the episcopal office theologically.

Finally, along the way the Church should continue to reflect on its understanding that episcopacy is not a third order. That bishops remain presbyters, that they do not constitute a third order, has been a constitutive Methodist affirmation. That conviction, as we noted in chapter 2, underlay Wesley's resolve to ordain. The arguments and understanding that Wesley drew from Lord Peter King and Bishop Edward Stillingfleet have been reaffirmed and reasserted in Methodist apologetics ever since.

We may, however, have reached a point where Wesley's convictions stand some testing. Our arrival at that point and the imperative for further reflection and perhaps even reconsideration of this precept may be necessitated by the changes we have made to our ordination policies and particularly by the ending of the transitional diaconate. Currently, because bishops have been ordained deacon and then elder before being consecrated and because those ordinations are not removed by their consecration, they bear diaconal and presbyterial identities in their exercise of the episcopal office. They continue to represent the deacon's and elder's roles. And they have fittingly claimed service, Word, Sacrament, and order as their charge. Their affirmation of their service responsibilities have been quite remarkable. Bishops in the future, bishops ordained elder under the 1996 protocols, will not have been ordained deacons, will not bear that identity in the exercise of their episcopal office, and will therefore not represent the fullness of our ministry. Might an ordination to episcopacy that is their consecration in a third order, be necessary to convey to them sacramentally and actually the responsibilities of oversight over the whole of the Church and its ministry? Alternatively United Methodism might reintroduce the transitional diaconate. One way or another it needs to consider how the wholeness of its ministry is represented and overseen.

Notes

1. Roy H. Short, *The Episcopal Leadership Role in United Methodism* (Nashville: Abingdon Press, 1985), p. 28.

2. *The Book of Discipline* 1992, Sect. 112, pp. 111-14; *Discipline* 1988, Sect. 112, pp. 116-18. In 1996, General Conference reduced that section to two short paragraphs, replacing it, in effect, by an extended discussion of "Servant Ministry and Servant Leadership." *Discipline* 1996, Sects. 109-16, pp. 109-12. For an excellent discussion of this section and its import, see Bruce W. Robbins, "Connection and *Koinonia*: Wesleyan and Ecumenical Perspectives on the Church," *Doctrines and Discipline: Methodist Theology and Practice*, vol. 3 of *United Methodism and American Culture*, eds. Dennis M. Campbell, William B. Lawrence, and Russell E. Richey (Nashville: Abingdon Press, 1999), pp. 197-212.

Structures of General Oversight

For more than a century, the UMC and its predecessor bodies have continued to affirm the general oversight responsibilities of itinerant general superintendency, while designating more and more of that oversight to lay and clergy councils. We propose that the UMC renew its episcopal ecclesiology by giving the bishops constitutional and legislative responsibility for inspiring and proposing missional directions for the denomination as a whole. This responsibility would be a concrete expression of the bishops' oversight, building on their initiatives of the last twenty years, and incorporating and expanding the duties of unwieldy conciliar bodies. Our proposal would express the nature of bishops' general oversight and their ordination to Word—recalling Christ's prophetic office.

In their 1995 proposal for *A New Connection*, Andy Langford and William Willimon urged that the Council of Bishops take over the functions of the General Council on Ministries (GCOM). The powers and duties of GCOM detailed in ¶ 906 would be transferred to the Council of Bishops as an extension of the bishops' conciliar "oversight of the spiritual and temporal affairs of the whole Church" grounded in the constitution and adumbrated in ¶ 427.3. These GCOM duties include the election of general secretaries of General Conference agencies, evaluation of general agency work, development of budget proposals for the general agencies in cooperation with the General Council on Finance and Administration (GCFA), and coordination of general church programs to synchronize calendars and eliminate overlap.

The GCOM was created as part of a reformed general agency structure adopted in the new United Methodist Church in 1972. Since the General Conference has no executive agency authorized to take action when it is not in session, the 1972 plan established a system of checks and balances through two councils of "review and oversight on behalf of the General Conference" (¶ 703.1). The GCOM is to "facilitate the church's program life as determined by the General Conference" (¶ 904), while GCFA is to manage all the general funds of the church (¶ 806). The *Discipline* mandates that the two councils work together to plan the quadrennial budget to be presented to General Conference. Yet the structure is clear in separating program and money so that, to put it bluntly, the people who want to run with program ideas cannot just write checks to pay for them, and the people who write the checks cannot block program initiatives that have been authorized by General Conference. This separation of authority builds accountability and trust, and is considered wise governance in any organization.

The viability of GCOM itself has never been as clear, however. Many people have expressed doubt that a group of laity, clergy, and bishops representing every jurisdiction in the United States and the central conferences could have enough time, information, and experience to carry out the responsibilities described in the *Discipline*. Even a major reduction in the size of GCOM membership in 1996 has not restored confidence. On the other hand, everyone has recognized the need for coordination of the work authorized by General Conference. The earlier program council and coordinating council forms in the predecessor denominations, the Methodist Church (MC) and Evangelical United Brethren Church (EUBC) are testimony to the Church's continuing need for some structure of general program coordination between sessions of General Conference.

Council of Bishops or General Council on Ministries?

The Council of Bishops (COB) currently has no constitutional or legislative authority for specific oversight of the general agencies. While the

Council is charged to conduct "regularized consultation and cooperation with other councils and service agencies of the Church" (¶ 427.3), the general agencies are not accountable to the Council of Bishops as a council. Rather, individual bishops serve as members of the general agencies, sharing information about the agencies through the Council meetings. The general secretaries attend Council meetings as well, occasionally to make presentations, but most often just to be available for consultation.

The lack of specific structures for the bishops' oversight responsibilities reflects the constitutional balance of powers between conference and episcopacy. General Conference has not tried to define the bishops' general church powers and duties beyond the broad mandate of the constitution. The bishops have the prerogative to fulfill these duties as they see fit. At the same time, General Conference has carefully defined the oversight powers and duties of its own agencies, GCOM and GCFA. Since these councils have individual bishops as members, and have specific responsibilities to fulfill in relation to all general agencies, the scope of action of the COB is severely circumscribed. The bishops as a council have oversight of the whole denomination, but no agency of General Conference is directly accountable to them. This leaves the substance of their conciliar oversight unstructured and indeterminate.

The question now is whether the COB ought to carry GCOM-type responsibilities under the constitutional separation and balance of powers. If general program agencies were accountable to the COB, the bishops' oversight would at once become more substantive and more restricted. The COB would have mandated duties of program coordination and evaluation, budgeting, and election of general secretaries. The COB would itself appear to be accountable to General Conference for the performance of COB duties, a constitutional relationship that has never existed.

The accountability relationship could run the other way around, however. General Conference could be viewed as giving over accountability for its own agencies to the COB. Because of the separation of powers, the COB would have the prerogative to carry out these duties in its own way. Moreover, the COB would have to be constitutionally authorized to propose legislative changes to general agency powers and duties. Otherwise the bishops would have no capacity for devising actions that they see as necessary to the advancement of general church ministries.

Taxing the Episcopal Office?

Were the COB to take on these specific oversight tasks, the episcopal role might be at risk of becoming more executive, as some commentators have been wont to call it all along. That is, the bishops might begin to look more like CEOs with general agency secretaries reporting to them. If they assumed the GCOM's task of negotiating general church budgets, they would also have to have a regular system of reviewing financial reports and assessing needs. The Council would need an even larger staff and office than is contemplated under the proposal for a four-year presidency. The sheer paperwork and staff support required to obtain the information necessary for evaluation and planning general agency activities and budgets would overwhelm a small office, and would be impossible under the current COB management system (that is to say, without any office at all). The COB would have to meet more often and the bishops would have to devote considerably more time to general church matters.

Such management duties could overshadow the bishops' pastoral role for the connection. The Church runs this risk in any strengthening of the bishops' roles within the denomination, but especially in plans that increase the bishops' powers vis-à-vis General Conference and/or the general agencies (i.e., in this proposal and the one that follows). More concretely, were a pyramidal executive structure to emerge, the whole denomination would be at risk legally. Civil courts would be able to interpret the UM connection as one continuous organizational hierarchy with the bishops as CEOs liable for the actions of all units reporting to them. A strongly worded constitutional statement on the nature of conciliar authority in the covenant community of the UMC would have to be devised to counteract such civil court readings of church polity. Such a statement would show that the bishops' powers are pastoral and conciliar, not executive, and that they function in balance with the powers of a delegate assembly, the General Conference.

The Bishops' Vision for Connectional Mission

Given these constitutional cautions, we argue that the Church should authorize the COB to exercise oversight of general church programs in more specific forms than just individual bishops' membership. Langford and Willimon's proposal that the powers and duties of GCOM simply be transferred to the COB raises too many constitutional issues. But the COB certainly could exercise more oversight duties than it does at present.

We propose that the "objectives" listed for GCOM (¶ 905) be assumed by the COB. These would include study of the missional needs of the general church, review and evaluation of program agency performance in fulfilling their ministries, and engaging in research and planning for the mission of the denomination as a whole. These responsibilities would put the COB at the forefront of new directions and initiatives, and give the bishops authority for general church leadership.

Many other duties currently designated to GCOM, such as minimizing overlapping and conflicting ministries, distributing responsibility among the agencies for implementing missional priorities, coordinating calendars, and reviewing General Conference resolutions, could be accomplished by a coordinating council comprised of the general secretaries, an equal number of bishops, and one lay or clergy member of each program agency (approximately thirty persons total). This body could also assemble the proposed budgets of the agencies and negotiate with GCFA a quadrennial financial asking to be proposed to General Conference, confirm the election of general secretaries by their respective agencies, and review agency plans for their facilities.

This plan gives the COB a vital role in studying, planning, and initiating the mission of the connection as a whole, while not burdening the COB with coordination tasks that more readily can be carried out by the persons directly involved in them. It also maintains the separation of fiscal responsibility from program administration. GCFA could continue as is, while GCOM as a separate entity would no longer be necessary. Funds that currently support the GCOM budget could be used to provide staff for the COB and the coordinating council of general secretaries, bishops, and agency members.

Constitutional Ways Forward

The COB as a distinct constitutional entity must have latitude to carry out its new responsibilities for general church mission in its own way. A constitutional amendment could be added as a second paragraph under ¶ 45, as a further specific authorization for the bishops' conciliar oversight of the whole Church:

> In its general oversight of the entire Church, the Council of Bishops shall study the missional needs of the whole Church, review and evaluate the performance of the general program agencies in fulfilling their ministries as authorized by General Conference, conduct research on the church's ministry and mission, and propose to General Conference initiatives for the mission of The United Methodist Church.

This amendment would not determine how the bishops fulfill their oversight responsibilities, but would give them authorization for initiatives on behalf of the whole Church. It would empower the bishops to bring proposals to General Conference and thus a structure and procedure through which they could have concrete influence on future directions of the UMC.

Enabling legislation for the coordinating council could be added to the General Provisions for agencies (Section I, ¶ 701 ff.), rather than replacing what is now GCOM legislation (¶ 901 ff.). This would emphasize that its duties are more restricted in range than those of GCFA. Its powers would be limited to coordination carried out as close as possible to actual agency decision-making, and its participants would be those actually responsible for program management.

The powers to evaluate, plan, and propose the missional program of the denomination as a whole connection would belong to the COB. This would resonate with The Methodist Church structure from 1939 to 1956 in which all bishops were members of the Board of Missions, thereby focusing their superintendency on the church's mission. The COB would not have exclusive powers to propose, by any means, since all general agencies would still seek improved ways to carry out their mandates, and any caucus, group, or individual United Methodist could still petition General Conference. But the Church would charge the bishops with a primary duty to advance the Church's future directions of witness and service through well-researched, balanced, and challenging proposals for action.

Theological Possibilities and Implications

Some of what was affirmed about the theology of the office in relation to our prior two proposals pertains also to this one. In particular, election of bishops by General Conference would make clearer the expectation that they exercise leadership of the whole connection and invite further theologizing about bishops as general superintendents. Even if United

Methodism does not opt for the episcopal roles outlined above, it has charged our bishops with significant general responsibilities. Our church models a distinctive style of episcopacy, one that warrants our conceptualizing and so sharing with the wider Christian family.

With its expectation that the bishops individually and collectively undertake the planning and missional direction of the Church, our style of episcopacy recalls Christ's prophetic office and the *Word* rubric for ministry. We can afford to mine the Scripture more consistently for our understanding of and rationale for episcopal leadership in the Church's outreach. Clearly, in this dimension of their work, the bishops and particularly the Council, have shown considerable passion and some remarkable successes. The COB's internal workings, teachings and missional initiatives, and various statements should offer much with which to work. Clearly, the COB does have a "word" for the Church. Clearly, also, its teachings and missional initiatives reflect a prophetic self-understanding. Should that be the centerpiece of United Methodist episcopacy, the point around which other functions and understandings revolve? There are precedents.

Prophetic roles, we noted, Asbury exercised along with his compatriot, Thomas Coke, in early American Methodism. They were the editors-in-chief, primary policymakers of the denomination, shapers and annotators of the *Discipline,* and coordinators of the Church's work. The Restrictive Rules indeed have protected our "itinerant general superintendency," but they also substantively altered the role that Francis Asbury had played as a connectional officer and in conference affairs. Asbury not only presided in annual and general conferences, but also served as the agenda setter, the policymover, and the agent of the church's mission.

The bishops have been self-conscious about the importance of "conferencing" and of their role as models thereof. This third pattern extends that responsibility throughout the whole of our structure and effectively makes the bishops our "general" conferencing agents. This recovery of the episcopal voice, and of the bishops collectively and individually, accents the general aspect of the Methodist understanding of *episkopē*. It evokes the *Word* as a basic ordination or ministerial rubric. And it recalls the prophetic dimension of Christ's office.

PROPOSAL 4

Superintendency and the Bishops' Role in Presiding

The United Methodist Church depends on its presiding officers, the bishops, to make forms of conference and Christian conversation possible in a diverse community. We propose that the Church further expand this crucial role. By enabling the bishops to preside in more settings and to be more activist in planning conference agendas, the Church will find its conferences more productive and more inspired. Our proposal offers a further embodiment of superintendency and expression of the bishops' ordination to Order—a living-out of Christ's kingly office.

The bishops have an essential place in conference work. As presiding officers without a voice in the content of matters being discussed, they attend primarily to the body's own rules for addressing the issues and proposals that come before it. For the sake of the good order of the Church, they suppress their own interests and do what they can to help the body achieve consensus for action. Through their fairness, their tone, and their choice of language, they have the opportunity to create a space in which Christian conversation and conferencing may occur.

The presiding role has only grown more significant in an increasingly diverse, multilingual, global Church comprised of persons from many cultures. The Church asks the bishops to be generous hosts, welcoming all voices and establishing an atmosphere of trust and mutuality across many lines of difference. As presiding officers, the bishops are frequently called upon to act on behalf of the body by mirroring back to an individual member or to the body the sense of what is being said or proposed, by insisting that members use language that is not accusatory, hyperbolic, or offensive, and by steering the body away from legislative or ideological quagmires toward constructive tasks. These presiding skills are more urgent than ever if the Methodist tradition of making decisions in conference, not in executive bodies, is to be sustained.

Presiding Opportunities

The challenge for the UMC now is to find ways to expand and enhance this crucial presiding role without detracting from it. Bishops are charged with presiding in all forms of UM conferences, that is, serving as presiding officers of actual conference sessions. But moreover, as a kind of extension of that presiding, they are mandated "to provide general oversight for the fiscal and program operations of the annual conference(s)." As in the general church, the *Discipline* provides no further guidelines for how this oversight is to be carried out. At the least, it must mean that the bishop should "ensure that the annual conference and general church policies and procedures are followed"—that is, by reminding conference units of their own rules and lines of amenability (¶ 415.1, .2). But many people rightly wonder if the presiding role cannot mean more than this.

The 1996 General Conference opened the way for annual conferences to organize their ministry and mission in their own way. Too many proposals for new annual conference structures, though, muddied the bishops' role by making the bishop a voting member of an executive or coordinating council or making conference units accountable to the bishop. Judicial Council has wisely overruled such proposals as violating the constitutional separation of powers between conference and episcopacy. Some proposals have been especially problematic in mixing amenability for program and money into the same oversight units including the bishop. These plans not only create unprecedented executive agencies of conferences, but also neglect the separation of program and financial management that is so important for creating collective trust and accountability in an organization. For the bishop to be a member of such an executive unit would completely contravene the episcopal presiding role.

We argue that conferences, whether annual or general, should build on the features of the presiding role itself. We see four directions in which presidency, already a central strength and dynamic of episcopacy, could be extended. First, conferences could ask bishops to preside in more venues than is presently the case. This would expand the episcopal role of hosting and enhancing conference as a community of discernment and decision. We welcome the plan of the 2004 committee for General Conference to ask bishops to preside over the legislative committees as well as the plenary sessions. Parallel presiding duties could be developed in annual conference sessions, such as meetings of the orders of elder and deacon, or orientation and discussion sessions for the lay members of conference. When conference is not in session, the bishops could be presiding officers of major annual conference units for program coordination and for finance such as conference councils, and in meetings or retreats of the clergy orders.

Second, greater coordination between the COB, the secretary of General Conference, and the general secretaries of agencies would allow for bishops to take a more active role in planning the agenda and process for General Conference. Especially at their fall and spring meetings immediately prior to General Conference, the bishops could assess the major issues and proposals coming forward from general agencies, examine the range of petitions from annual conferences, local churches, and individuals, and anticipate how to expedite healthy discussion and decision on the myriad matters that come to the conference sessions.

Third, conferences need to create more avenues through which bishops could articulate their appraisal of current ministry and mission and offer insights, challenges, and visions for future directions. At the moment, such opportunities are confined to the episcopal address at General Conference or occasional "state of the Church" speeches at annual conferences. Individual bishops have many opportunities to interpret church issues and inspire church members to new visions of the church's ministries. But these individual moments lack continuity. If the bishops in council assume the planning objectives of the current GCOM structure for the general church, they will need a regular venue through which to report their appraisals and make proposals for conference action. Their proposals would then enter the legislative process like any others for consideration.

If bishops individually and collectively do become more active in proposing legislation, they will have to redouble their efforts to be consistent, fair, and hospitable in presiding over conferences. To avoid even the appearance of a conflict of interest, they must not confuse their moments of presiding with their occasions of presenting or advocating. Here might be an opportunity for bishops to revive the long-standing tradition of exchanging their presidential duties. In an annual conference, on the day a bishop has a place in the agenda for presenting and interpreting a proposal, a bishop from another episcopal area or a bishop from that region but a different Wesleyan or Anglican tradition could preside. In General Conference, on the day the COB presents its assessment of current directions and proposals for future ministry and mission, a bishop from another Wesleyan or Anglican tradition could preside. This would be both a useful and a symbolic practice for showing the origin and extent of the ecumenical Wesleyan heritage and its signature form of conference.

Picture, for example, a bishop presenting to the annual conference over which she presides a plan for starting ten new local churches in the coming year. The African Methodist Episcopal bishop from that area is in the chair. A lively discussion ensues, grounded in extensive conversations that have already occurred in conference task groups and councils. The conversation is enriched through the visible presence of another tradition in the chair. When the conference acts to support the plan, the AME bishop announces that he is going to propose a similar plan in his conference. The vitality of the Church is stirred, affirmed, and celebrated in such moments.

Fourth, the bishops in council could also extend the presiding role that the Church so depends upon, into wider efforts to model healthy communication in church systems. The COB could engage in a continuous process of responding to questions and issues through a publication or Web site. They could have a conciliar office of communications that could answer queries from the secular and religious press. Through reading and awareness of newsletters, Web sites, online chat rooms, and publications, they could alert the connection to useful resources and constructive approaches to ministry and mission in the Wesleyan tradition. They could anticipate controversies stirred up by exaggerated claims and incorrect information, clarifying Church actions and laying rumors to rest.

Filling a Communications Vacuum

Such an expanded communications role, together with modeling of judicious and balanced interpretations of issues, would fill what is largely a vacuum in denominational life today. The UMC has no collective voice when General Conference is not in session. The General Board of Church and Society is highly visible as it carries out its mandate "to seek the implementation of the Social Principles" through "forthright witness and action" (¶ 1004). Other general agencies may issue statements on particular issues, making clear that they speak only under their own mandates and are not going beyond the authority of General Conference as the Church's official voice. No single body of the general church has the authority on behalf of the whole Church to address either crisis situations or accusations and agendas of well-organized political action groups. No agency of the general church can step forward on behalf of the whole Church to sponsor conversation that moves beyond sound bites, or to insist on balanced presentations of the facts about church trends or conference actions.

The COB could play this role of enhanced communications and improved conversation in the Church without trespassing on General Conference prerogatives. The bishops would not have to go beyond the resolutions or standards issued by General Conference, only to interpret them and help the Church think about how to implement them. The bishops could also do what General Conference cannot do, which is to sustain direct communication, reliable data, and constructive exchanges of views over the entire quadrennium between conference sessions.

But the bishops have had too little collective voice to this point. Two meetings a year eventuate in a handful of statements about whatever world issue is current at that moment. The UMC needs a public, conciliar, episcopal voice to establish a more consistent framework for conversation and exchange of information and ideas when conferences are not in session. This could be one crucial task of an office of the COB, building upon and extending the bishops' traditional role of presiding over conference and enabling the best possible Christian conversation.

A Theology of Superintendency

Our final proposal evokes Christ's royal office, *order* as ministerial or ordination rubric, and the presiding or superintending dimension of episcopacy. It recalls the preeminent role that Asbury played in setting agenda for conferences and, by his appointments, setting agenda for circuits and stations. Asbury chaired in active fashion, bringing in proposals, making motions, speaking to matters under discussion. While William McKendree's innovation of the episcopal address recalled that earlier role, it did so in quite minimal fashion. Post-1808, one might say, bishops in conference lost their voice, being expected to speak only when spoken to, that is, to preside only.

While bishops have hardly been voiceless, their presidency might to advantage be restored to its Asburian activism. And Asbury's own self-understanding, reflected especially in the annotated *Discipline* of 1798, ought to be an important resource for and conversational piece in our rethinking superintendency. The authoritarian streaks in Asbury, however, do not need to be reclaimed and, impressions to the contrary notwithstanding, do not comport well with the superintending, ordering, and royal dimension of episcopacy. The best antidote to such distortions and key to an apt theology of the ordering or royal role is a close reading of the Scripture and of Christ's exercise of his office. One could do worse than start the discussion of order and episcopacy with Philippians 2.

For this dimension of episcopacy, we can learn much also from other traditions and from ecumenical discussions of the threefold office of ministry and of *episkopē*. United Methodists will not, for reasons already advanced, wish to emulate our Episcopal kinfolk either in thinking in diocesan terms about the episcopal office or modeling the COB after the House of Bishops. However, the current conversations about the office in the U.S. between United Methodists and Episcopalians can be of help, as also the earlier discussions between United Methodists and Lutherans.[1] So too, the various multilateral discussions, including those from Faith and Order: "Baptism, Eucharist and Ministry" and "The Nature and Purpose of the Church: A Stage on the Way to a Common Statement."[2]

Such ecumenical statements need to be balanced by careful development of our connectional and conferencing ecclesial principles and the situating of episcopacy therein. We as United Methodists have much to contribute and much to gain from ecumenical conversations. We need to claim the distinctiveness and theological import of our episcopacy, in its ordering roles, as also in the various dimensions of our plan of itinerant general superintendency. It is time that we overcome our own theological inhibitions with regard to episcopacy, challenge other denominations' discount of our theological prowess, and undertake a full-fledged theology of the office.

Notes

1. Jack M. Tuell and Roger W. Fjeld, eds., *Episcopacy: Lutheran-United Methodist Dialogue II* (Minneapolis: Augsburg, 1991).

2. "The Nature and Purpose of the Church: A Stage on the Way to a Common Statement," Faith and Order Paper No. 181—November 1998; World Council of Churches, Faith and Order; http://www.wcc-coe.org/wcc/what/faith/nature.html, especially the section "Oversight: Communal, Personal and Collegial" and "Baptism, Eucharist, and Ministry," Faith and Order Paper No. 111. World Council of Churches; http://www.wcc-coe.org/wcc/what/faith/bem5.html.

POSTSCRIPT

The time is long past due for United Methodism to undertake serious study and discussion of its episcopacy. The Church needs to review the trends of the past thirty years, to see how the polity and practice of episcopacy has been evolving, and to discern directions for the future. This is a study that General Conference should authorize, but in which bishops, district superintendents, clergy, and laity from across the Church must be active participants. Through such a study and the proposals that result from it, the Church will have a chance to realize the full potential of its episcopacy for leading the Church into a new century.

A lot of energy for defining how episcopacy was to be practiced went into the church union discussions that created The Methodist Church in 1939 and The United Methodist Church in 1968. But no record of how differences were reconciled is apparent to today's reader of the *Discipline*. All that remains is the bold constitutional sentence stating that "there shall be a continuance of an episcopacy in The United Methodist Church," that this episcopacy will have the "plan, powers, privileges, and duties" like those of predecessor denominations, and that "the differences between these historic episcopacies are deemed to be reconciled and harmonized" (¶ 43).

The *Discipline* provides no theological or ecclesiological rationale for episcopacy in the UMC; does not locate UM episcopacy in the spectrum of episcopal practices in various Christian traditions; and defines few specifically mandated responsibilities of bishops. While a number of bishops have

145

published autobiographies or been the subject of biographical studies, few have attempted their own interpretation of any theological or historical basis for their role in the Church.

Our book is one of very few in recent generations to address the historical and theological foundations of United Methodist episcopacy. It follows the recent publications of James Kirby's history and of James Mathews and William Oden's Council of Bishops documents. Almost forty years have passed since Gerald Moede's monograph, and in the intervening time only a very few discussions of episcopacy, such as those of James Mathews and Roy Short, have been attempted. General Conference has not sponsored a study of superintendency, general and district, since the 1960s and 1970s.

In the nineteenth century many Methodist clergy and scholars mounted vigorous defenses of episcopacy as the Methodists practiced it, attempting to show Wesley's intentions and wise use of patristic sources and to demonstrate that episcopacy could fit with the emerging American democracy. By contrast, today's Church is largely silent on the matter. Could this be in part because episcopacy is simply taken for granted, not controversial, proceeding without comment or criticism from outside Methodist traditions, and in any case greatly restricted in scope and powers from earlier days?

We believe The United Methodist Church must undertake more research, discussion, and envisioning of the episcopal role in the Church. United Methodist episcopacy needs to be located among practices of episcopacy in various Christian traditions, and to be given grounding in the nature and purpose of the Church. This is particularly important today as the use of the title "bishop" proliferates among pastors of independent Pentecostal and evangelical congregations. Even some churches with the word "Baptist" in their names, which one would assume to be a marker of stringent Protestant refusal of ritual pomp and ecclesiastical hierarchy, have a pastor with the title "bishop," anointed, consecrated, or ordained to this role (language varies) within his (mainly his) own congregation. These congregations (like King and Stillingfleet, discussed in chapter 2) claim to find a basis for this practice in the New Testament. They are clearer about the grounds for episcopacy in their congregations than United Methodists typically are about the basis for the office of bishop in UM traditions.

General Conference should sponsor a study of superintendency in the UMC, including historical and theological discussions, surveys of the practices of superintendency among bishops and district superintendents, and proposals for enhancing the effectiveness of the office for the future of the Church. Almost no data on how superintendency is actually being carried out is readily available. Scholarly and/or pastoral discussions of superintendency, either general or district (but especially the latter) are sparse. Past studies have tended toward a narrow focus on issues around ordination and appointments, with little attention finally being given to the broader nature of the superintending offices. Perhaps now the Church is ready for a fresh effort to collect information and to envision an enhanced and expanded episcopal role in the Church.

In short, in our view the church should give a lot of thought and study to issues of episcopacy before it acts. We know the cynics will say, "Oh no, not another commission-to-study . . . !" But we have provided four options, with some discussion of attendant issues, and would hope that serious attention to our effort might indeed be helpful should the Church decide to act at this General Conference. Our counsel, however, would be to defer or take minimal action, to study first, perhaps starting with what we and others have written, and to prepare the Church as a whole over the next quadrennium for a new chapter with a reinvigorated episcopacy.